WORLD HERITAGE SITES

Genevieve Wheatley

ENGLISH HERITAGE

CONTENTS

The remains of the Mayan city at Tikal, Guatemala, a cultural World Heritage Site. This site is also inscribed on the World Heritage List as a natural site because of its position in an area of unspoilt tropical rainforest.

ABOUT THIS BOOK

As a species we seem fascinated with our past. As part of a Western cultural and, so-called, *scientific* tradition we have catalogued and categorised the known past into chronological periods that emphasise great events and people. We tend to latch on to the impressive physical achievements of the past and identify them almost as goals at which to aim in the future.

Much of the thought that permeates modern Western culture has its roots in ancient Greece where, by the second or third century BC, writers had identified Seven Wonders of the World. These Wonders were acknowledged to be magnificent achievements of not only ancient technology but also ancient culture and thought. Today, only the Pyramids of Egypt survive from the original list, that also included the Hanging Gardens of Babylon, the Mausoleum of Halicarnassus, the Pharos of Alexandria, the Temple of Artemis at Ephesus, the Statue of Zeus at Olympia and the Colossus of Rhodes.

In 1972 UNESCO (the United Nations Educational, Scientific and Cultural Organisation) adopted the Convention concerning the Protection of the World Cultural and Natural Heritage (see page 4) which allowed for the creation of a List of natural and cultural sites that are of *outstanding universal value*. The cultural sites of this World Heritage List can, in many ways, be looked upon as the modern equivalent of the Greek Wonders. The List is an international acknowledgement of the significance of those buildings, monuments and sites inscribed on it as well as a statement of the importance, *for all the peoples of the world*, of safeguarding them. Those writing of the cultural sites and monuments on the List talk of

The Pyramid of Chephren at Giza. The Pyramids of Egypt are the only remaining ancient Wonder of the World.

a common world heritage created through the 'genius of mankind' and a common responsibility to preserve this heritage for future generations in a belief that the sites and monuments can themselves help us to understand what it means to be human. It is a huge task.

This book concentrates on the cultural sites on the World Heritage List and describes briefly the international organisation that supports the List. It then uses a series of examples from the United Kingdom and elsewhere to highlight many of the problems that face these modern wonders including conflicting claims over the ownership of, and control over, cultural property, pollution, war damage and the pressure of increased tourism. It argues that all pupils should have a knowledge of the World Heritage Convention and List and it suggests ways in which such a study can be introduced into the curriculum. In doing so it raises questions as to the value of keeping such a List and what it tells us about both the

monuments of the past and about our modern preoccupation with them.

For most educational purposes cultural World Heritage Sites are no different from any other historic site and the full range of educational approaches can be used as suggested in numerous general publications produced by English Heritage or published specifically in relation to particular sites (see Bibliography and resources). However, because of their special status, World Heritage Sites do provide very good examples for many of the issues surrounding the protection, preservation and presentation of the physical remains of the past. Most of these issues are cross-curricular. The suggested educational links are by no means exhaustive and teachers will be able to add to them with ideas to suit their own particular situations.

THE WORLD HERITAGE CONVENTION

WHAT IS THE WORLD HERITAGE CONVENTION?

In 1972 UNESCO adopted the Convention concerning the Protection of the World Cultural and Natural Heritage. The Convention came into force in 1975 and has now been ratified by 147 countries. It is concerned with the identification, protection, conservation and presentation of those parts of the world's natural and cultural heritage that are of *outstanding universal value*. While the Convention explicitly links sites of natural and cultural heritage, arguing that the cultural achievements of the past took place within specific natural landscapes and reminding humanity of the fundamental need to preserve the balance between humanity and the natural environment, this book concentrates on the cultural sites on the World Heritage List.

There is no attempt within the Convention to suggest that the past can be re-lived or that the appreciation of the monuments of the past should be used to revive obsolete values or beliefs. Nor does it commend one civilization or culture above another. Rather it attempts to draw attention to the wide range of human creativity that has left its mark on the landscape. In effect the Convention implies the rejection of political history and the development of a universally agreed policy for the protection of the achievements of the past.

The Convention is a legal instrument through which countries (Known as *States Parties* to the Convention) voluntarily commit themselves to safeguarding those places that they nominate for inclusion on the World Heritage

The conical tower in the Great Enclosure at the World Heritage Site of Great Zimbabwe, Zimbabwe (see page 18).

List. Nominations for the List are considered by an inter-governmental World Heritage Committee (see below).

The Convention also recognises that many of the world's cultural masterpieces are under increasing threat of damage or outright destruction and that they are frequently situated in developing countries unable to cope with the financial pressures of protection, conservation or preservation. Hence, those states that have signed the Convention have committed themselves, at least in principle, to assisting the less wealthy signatories in preserving the World Heritage Sites that lie within their modern national borders. This is achieved by The World Heritage Committee administering a World Heritage Fund to which all States Parties contribute. The Fund, which is extremely small, is usually used to pay for training, specialist advice or equipment for major conservation or restoration projects, usually in the less developed countries.

The World Heritage List

Sites proposed for inclusion on the World Heritage List are nominated by one of the States Parties to the Convention. The nominations are considered by the World Heritage Committee which is made up of representatives of 21 of the countries that have ratified the Convention, who are elected on a rota basis. However, before the Committee considers nominations it seeks advice from one of two non-governmental organisations: the International Council of Monuments and Sites (ICOMOS) for cultural nominations and the World Conservation Union (IUCN) for natural nominations. Occasionally, for example when a site is nominated as a Cultural Landscape (see page 6) both organisations are consulted. With respect to cultural sites ICOMOS consults with specialists with a particular knowledge of the site and its history and sends one or more experts to study the present condition of the site and the steps already undertaken to protect and conserve it. An evaluation of the 'outstanding universal value' of the site and a recommendation as to whether or not it should be added to the List is then presented to the World Heritage Committee for consideration.

The long-term intention of the List is to create an inventory of natural and cultural sites that is as comprehensive, representative and coherent as possible. The existence of the List, however, does not mean that all important cultural sites should necessarily be added to it. To be added to the List a site has to be of outstanding *international* importance. There are many thousands of sites that are extremely important at a local, national or regional level that will never be included on the List. However, it is certainly the hope of those involved in drawing up the List that its mere existence will focus attention on the need to preserve, conserve and present all important cultural heritage, whether it is on the List or not.

The criteria for a cultural monument or site to be selected are that it should satisfy one or more of the following:

■ 'Constitute a masterpiece of human creative genius

■ Have exercised considerable influence at a certain period or within a cultural area of the world

■ Provide exceptional evidence of a culture which is living or has disappeared

■ Illustrate a significant historical period

■ Constitute an outstanding example of a traditional way of life

■ Be associated with ideas or beliefs of a universal significance'.

The Convention defines three types of cultural sites:

■ 'monuments: architectural works, works of monumental sculpture and painting, elements or structures of an archaeological nature, inscriptions, cave dwellings and combinations of features, which are of outstanding universal value from the point of view of history, art or science;

■ groups of buildings: groups of separate or connected buildings which, because of their architecture, their homogeneity or their place in the landscape, are of outstanding universal value from the point of view of history, art or science;

■ sites: works of man[sic] or the combined works of nature and man[sic], and areas including archaeological sites which are of outstanding universal value from the historical, aesthetic, ethnological or anthropological points of view.'

The addition of a site or monument to the List does not provide it with any extra formal international legal protection. However, it does ensure significant international prestige for a site and provides an avenue to international support and the possibility of limited funding through the World Heritage Fund. It also significantly raises the profile of the site within its own country as, by nominating a site or monument for inclusion on the List, countries are explicitly stating their commitment to the ideal of a world heritage and the importance of the protection and conservation of the monuments that together make up that heritage. Inclusion on the List has certainly stimulated governments – or their advisory agencies – to look in greater detail at the management of sites on the List and to at least attempt where necessary to increase provision for their protection and conservation.

It has become increasingly clear that the work of the World Heritage Committee should not stop once a site or monument has been inscribed on the List, but rather that a programme of monitoring needs to be implemented to chart the continued protection and conservation of the site. Such a programme allows for a constant consultative process between site managers, government officials and regional or world experts made available through the monitoring programme. The implementation of a monitoring programme has therefore become part of the

The Aswan High Dam: the threat that began it all

In 1960 the Egyptian government received Soviet funding to build the Aswan High Dam. The dam, which was completed in 1970, was intended to control the annual flooding of the Nile thereby providing much needed irrigation and hydroelectric power for Egypt and the Sudan. It was immediately obvious that the resulting reservoir would permanently flood a number of important ancient Nubian sites and, as it was clear that neither Egypt nor the Sudan could themselves finance a rescue programme, the then Director-General of UNESCO, René Maheu, launched an international appeal to save the monuments.

Some $80 million were raised to finance one of the most remarkable heritage projects ever undertaken as five groups of temples were dismantled, restored and re-erected on new sites. The most impressive of the temples, those of Ramesses II at Abu Simbel, had a 38m (125ft) facade fronting a 63m (207ft) sanctuary cut into solid rock.

The international co-operation stimulated by this rescue project provided a sympathetic environment for the development of the cultural aspects of the World Heritage Convention which was adopted by UNESCO in 1972, just four years after the temples of Ramesses II were relocated.

The temples of Ramesses II at Abu Simbel being reconstructed at their new location away from the flooding caused by the creation of the Aswan High Dam.

Operational Guidelines for sites accepted onto the List and all States Parties are now required to present a report every five years on the state of conservation of sites within their borders. Taken together with the original nomination documentation and the associated ICOMOS recommendation to the World Heritage Committee, these monitoring reports will provide a long term picture of the conservation of the site and should help in the identification of conservation problems before they become critical. It is hoped that the allocation of the limited resources of the World Heritage Fund for technical assistance, training and education programmes, and for the design of large scale investment projects will be helped enormously by such monitoring.

CULTURAL LANDSCAPES: A NEW DEVELOPMENT

A number of sites on the List have been nominated as both cultural and natural sites, for example at Tikal, in Guatemala, where the remains of one of the most important Mayan city states are included in an area of tropical rainforest. However, it was only in 1992 that the World Heritage Committee confirmed that it would accept nominations specifically for cultural landscapes. There are three categories:

■ 'clearly defined landscapes, designed and created intentionally by man [sic]

■ organically evolved continuing or fossil landscapes

■ landscapes justifiable by virtue of the powerful religious, artistic or cultural associations of the natural element rather than material cultural evidence, which may be significant or even absent.'

The first cultural landscape to be inscribed on the list was Tongariro, New Zealand. The natural features of Tongariro are an integral part of Maori mythology in which the mountains are deemed to be sacred. The area is now a National Park run jointly by the Department of Conservation and Maori people. The park is also unique as the first area to be donated by an indigenous group (in 1887) to a colonial power for the explicit purpose of protecting the religious elements of the area.

Other areas that are under consideration for nomination as cultural landscapes include the land associated with Cistercian abbeys in Europe. In this example the existence of some of the highest densi-

---

THE WORLD HERITAGE COMMITTEE SPEAKS OUT AGAINST WAR-INFLICTED DAMAGE

Declaration of the General Assembly of the States Parties (ninth session, 29–30 October 1993)
The General Assembly adopted the following declaration and requested that it be widely diffused:

'The representatives of the States Parties to the World Heritage Convention, meeting at UNESCO on 29 and 30 October 1993, in the framework of their General Assembly:
Express their grave concern in the face of the multiplication of risks brought about by armed conflict, turmoil and acts of terrorism, which increasingly threaten the very existence of the world cultural and natural properties;
Urgently request all States Parties to the Convention to make use of the media, to strengthen educational programmes and cultural events, and to encourage all populations world-wide to respect the cultural and natural heritage of their fellow men'.

World Heritage Committee Declaration Cartagena, December 1993
'The World Heritage Committee, representing the 136 States Parties to the Convention Concerning the Protection of the World Cultural and Natural Heritage, strongly supports the appeals of the Director-General and the General Conference of UNESCO to halt all destruction of the heritage of Bosnia-Herzegovina and to allow the international community to participate in the restoration work which is absolutely necessary.

The Committee vigorously condemns such destruction, like those which recently affected Mostar – in flagrant contradiction with international law – and urges the Director-General of UNESCO to send, as soon as the situation allows, the mission of experts requested by the General Conference in order to evaluate the damage and to study the possibility of providing emergency assistance'.

A view of some of the damage in Dubrovnik, Croatia added to the World Heritage in Danger List in 1991 after its targeting in the war in former Yugoslavia.

Jasenka Zavela-Spivalo

THREATS TO WORLD HERITAGE SITES

World Heritage Sites are subject to a wide range of both natural and human threats. Some problems arise from the economic development of countries and the associated industrialisation, pollution and population change. The threat to the temple of Ramesses II (see page 5) is a clear example of this type of problem. Other problems include the results of years of neglect, lack of finance or deliberate destruction – be it from colonial power, local people, individual collectors of antiquities or their agents. Some sites have been the victims of natural disasters, for example, the earthquake damaged old city of Cairo. Others, such as the historic centre of Florence, have been damaged by modern conflict, in this case a politically motivated car bomb. Unfortunately cultural sites are often prime targets during wars – as, for example, in the recent conflict in the former Yugoslavia where many cultural sites were specifically targeted by the warring factions including the World Heritage Site of Dubrovnik (see page 20). However, perhaps one of the greatest threats to World Heritage Sites has been through the increase in mass tourism – a threat frequently encouraged by a site's inclusion on the List (see pages 22-24).

World Heritage in Danger List

The World Heritage Committee can add any site on the List to a special World Heritage in Danger List. Sites on the Danger List can receive a variety of emergency aid, including the possibility of financial assistance from the World Heritage Fund and the raising of their particular problems within the international community. For example, the historic city of Dubrovnik was added to the Danger List in 1991 as a result of its shelling in the war in former Yugoslavia.

The Royal Palaces of Abomey II, Benin, were added to the Danger List immediately when they were added to the main World Heritage List in 1985. The Palaces form the only remaining evidence for one of the most powerful West African kingdoms of the nineteenth century, which was not only an integral part of the slave trade but also an early example of the centralised state in this part of Africa. The palaces were under threat from termites and erosion caused by rain and made worse by lack of maintenance. At present they are used as a living museum about the kingdom where, in addition to the usual functions of a museum, local people still go to perform religious ceremonies linked to the power of the old kings. As the remains were on the Danger List it was possible to set up an integrated maintenance programme for the site which included the essential element of training local staff to be able to carry out maintenance in the future. An associated element of the programme is to enable the local staff to integrate the site and its museum into tourist itineraries so as to make the site more self-sufficient financially.

Some of the mountains at Tongariro, New Zealand, part of the first Cultural Landscape to be inscribed on the World Heritage List.

ties of associated medieval remains – including not only the abbeys and their precincts but also outlying field systems, barns, cellars, sheep pens, mills, ovens, tile and glass works – raise enormous conservation problems as modern development and land use requirements destroy the historic environment.

One of the royal palaces of Abomey II, Benin. The palaces were added to the World Heritage in Danger List at the same time as they were inscribed on the World Heritage List in 1985 (see above).

THE IDENTIFICATION OF CULTURAL SITES IN THE UNITED KINGDOM

IDENTIFICATION AND NOMINATION OF SITES

The 1972 Convention was ratified by the United Kingdom in 1984. In 1985 a joint committee with representatives from all four countries of the United Kingdom identified a tentative list for consideration with a view to nominating one or two sites to the World Heritage Committee annually. To-date sixteen sites relating to the United Kingdom have been inscribed on the List including two natural sites in overseas UK Dependencies. Twelve of the United Kingdom sites are cultural sites, ten of which are in England. The twelve cultural sites are described between pages 10 and 15.

The drawing up of a United Kingdom list of potential nominations for submission to the World Heritage Committee is officially the responsibility of the Department of National Heritage. The Department consults with the Scottish, Welsh and Northern Ireland Offices and the Foreign and Commonwealth Office (for the dependant territories) and is advised by the various national agencies with responsibility for the heritage, of which the principal one, with respect to cultural sites in England, is English Heritage.

The Department and English Heritage continue to work with other relevant organisations and experts with a view to the possible nomination of further sites to the World Heritage Committee. Given ICOMOS's role as main advisor to the World Heritage Committee with respect to cultural sites, English Heritage and the Department work extremely closely with the UK National

The nomination documentation for Greenwich to become a World Heritage Site.

Committee of ICOMOS, which itself convenes a specialist panel to review sites for possible nomination.

In order to comply with the Convention the Department of National Heritage is keen that any future nominations:

■ are very selective and reflect the genuinely international importance of the site or monument in question, thus reflecting the fact that there must be a limit to the number of sites which meet UNESCO's criteria of 'Outstanding universal value'.

■ have adequate regard to the coherence of the nominated area for management purposes.

THE MANAGEMENT OF SITES

The Department of National Heritage, supported by the various national agencies with responsibility for the heritage, argues that little or no benefit would come from increased national legislation for World Heritage Sites within the UK. The results of a number of recent Public Inquiries that have safeguarded sites on the List from inappropriate development tend to support this view (see pages 29 to 31). Because of their importance, sites nominated by the UK for inclusion on the List are already protected by the strictest of legislation that is likely to be passed by Parliament in the foreseeable future. In the United Kingdom legal protection is achieved through the Listing of historic buildings and the Scheduling of ancient monuments, by the establishment of Conservation Areas, and by the outstanding international importance being taken into account as a key consideration by local planning authorities (see Bibliography and resources).

The Government also argues that sites should be seen as integral parts of local and regional conservation, tourist and development

On behalf of the Air Photographs Librarian RCHME, © Crown copyright

Aerial photograph of Maritime Greenwich showing the Royal Naval College on the banks of the River Thames to the north of the site. The Queen's House and the Royal Park to the south. Greenwich town centre and the Cutty Sark lie to the west.

plans and that they should not be perceived as intrusive islands of conservation' imposed from above. It is therefore the explicit intention that local government take responsibility for sites under its jurisdiction as it will only be through such an approach that the sites will become part of the local and regional planning process. This approach is crucial to all sites but is probably especially important for those sites such as Canterbury and Durham where, for example, it would be inappropriate to ban all development within or close to the designated sites as these areas form integral parts of living cities.

The Government is also aware, however, that there are severe pressures on nearly all of the sites both on the List and under consideration for nomination – some of which are outside the control or influence of local government – and it is keen that the UK gives an exemplary lead in the management and protection of these sites. Thus, the Department and English Heritage are encouraging the development of detailed management plans, that incorporate the views of all those bodies that have a legitimate interest in the sites. As combined policies for short- and long-term

management and planning strategy, these Plans should prove very effective as they will be able to address all factors potentially affecting any particular site. The Department of National Heritage is also encouraging all those responsible for the management of sites on the List to organise the effective monitoring of their sites in order to comply with the revised World Heritage Committee's Operational Guidelines.

> 'With regard to the more general question of World Heritage Sites, they are of widely differing kinds. Blenheim is, for example, a single historic site, whereas Bath is a complete city. Durham is a great Cathedral in a city, whereas Stonehenge is a site set in an archaeological landscape. It is therefore impossible to lay down specific rules for world heritage sites as different forms of approach are needed for each management plan.'
>
> Lord Montagu of Beaulieu, speaking in a House of Lords debate on World Heritage Sites on 21 October 1993.

The Department of National Heritage and all of the national heritage agencies are fully aware of the complexities of site management and are keen that all sites develop suitable management plans (see pages 32 to 34).

English Heritage Photo Library

The main circle at Avebury, Wiltshire which forms part of a World Heritage Site with other prehistoric monuments including Stonehenge.

THE CULTURAL SITES OF THE UNITED KINGDOM

It is impossible in such a short space to give anything but a very brief description of the cultural World Heritage Sites in the UK. More detailed publications concerning the sites are listed in the Bibliography and resources.

Blenheim Palace

Blenheim Palace is named after the Battle of Blenheim (1704) which was the first major victory for England in the War of the Spanish Succession. It was built by a grateful Queen Anne shortly after the victory as a reward for the English general John Churchill, Duke of Marlborough. Blenheim was the first of four major victories during the War of the Spanish Succession that broke the domination of Europe by France and ensured that England (and then Britain) became the leading European power for most of the next century. The Palace also has strong historical connections with Winston Churchill who was born there in 1874. He is buried nearby in Bladon parish church.

The Palace is situated in a large park. It was designed and built by Sir John Vanbrugh between 1705 and 1725. Vanbrugh based his designs on Palladio and, in a statement of architectural fashion tinged with some ironic humour, the Palace of Versailles in France – the architectural masterpiece of Louis XIV whose European power was broken by Marlborough. A centrepiece of the design is a Doric column on which the British lion mauls the French cockerel! The interior has a number of carvings by Gibbons and Hawksmoor.

Blentheim Palace

Blenheim Palace.

The large park was later landscaped by Capability Brown in the 1760s where, according to the famous landscape historian W G Hoskins, he created the 'most magnificent private lake in the country by damming the little river Glyme'.

Canterbury Cathedral, St Augustine's Abbey and St Martin's Church

Canterbury Cathedral is the seat of the Archbishop of Canterbury, the head of the world-wide Anglican Church. This, coupled with numerous historical associations, including the murder of St Thomas a Becket and subsequent public penance by Henry II in 1170, has made it a centre of religious pilgrimage for centuries. Canterbury was the base for the early Christian missionaries sent by Pope Gregory I in AD 597 from Rome, under the leadership of St Augustine who was the first Archbishop of Canterbury. When the missionaries arrived in

England, King Ethelbert of Kent, who was one of the prime political targets for conversion, allowed them to worship with his wife Bertha, who had been a Frankish Princess and was already a

Canterbury Cathedral with the remains of St Augustine's Abbey in the foreground.

Christian, in the old Roman church of St Martin's in Canterbury. Augustine founded the abbey that now bears his name about AD 598.

The cathedral, strictly known as Christchurch Cathedral, was begun in the eleventh century although most of the present building dates from no earlier than the fourteenth century. It is one of the most impressive of the English cathedrals. The ruins of nearby St Augustine's Abbey include remains from the seventh century onwards. Elements of the original Roman church can still be seen in St Martin's church.

Castles and town walls of King Edward in Gwynedd, Wales

The four castles, of Beaumaris, Caernarvon, Conway and Harlech, that make up this World Heritage Site were all built in the late thirteenth century by the English King Edward I as part of his campaigns to subjugate the Welsh. They are

Beaumaris castle, one of the four castles built by Edward I of England to subjugate the Welsh which together form a World Heritage Site.

direct physical evidence of the violent past of the United Kingdom. As royal projects, the castles have extremely full building records which add to their historical significance. Conway Castle's records are particularly complete and we are able to build up a picture of how the total construction cost of over £14,500 was made up, for example, each of the 142 arrow-slits were made by one John Flauner at a cost of 1s 2d each.

All four castles were probably designed by the same architect, James of St George from Savoy and combine three elements of military architecture that were major developments of their time. The castles:

■ dispensed with the usual Norman central strong tower, or keep, replacing it with a rectangular or polygonal curtain wall containing a series of symmetrically placed towers

■ included an extra outer curtain wall that, taken with the inner curtain wall, created a linked, double defense

■ included an immensely strong gatehouse, on the castle's most vulnerable side, into which all of the most up-to-date defensive technology was crammed.

It is the combination of these three elements that make the Edwardian castles in Wales the most impressive European military architecture of the thirteenth and fourteenth centuries.

While extremely expensive to build, the castles were far more cost-effective than a number of long and drawn out field campaigns – the only other means of subjugation. Once fully operational, Harlech castle withstood a siege from the entire Welsh army garrisoned by only 37 men. The castles also brought a long period of stability to Wales during which the economy blossomed, much to the relief of the English Exchequer.

City of Bath

Today Bath is the most complete, elegant and beautiful Georgian city in the United Kingdom. There are nearly 5000 Listed Buildings in the city that attract various levels of protection from alteration or demolition. These include the Pump Rooms, neo-classical facades and monuments, Queen Square, the Circus and the Royal

The Royal Crescent and the Circus, Bath. Designed by John Wood in the eighteenth century.

Crescent. Bath also has a number of landscaped parks. It is unique on the List in that the whole city was designated as a World Heritage Site rather than just significant historical sections of the city.

The city has its roots in a number of small prehistoric settlements that were consumed by the Roman spa city of Aquae Sulis. The Romans assimilated Sulis, the local goddess of healing, into their own cult of healing centred around the goddess Minerva. The Roman Bath House and Temple to Sulis-Minerva can still be visited. Bath was chosen by the Romans as a centre for healing because of the springs there which produce water naturally heated to some 120°F at a rate of nearly 250,000 gallons a day. It was these same springs which made Bath a favourite spa resort in the medieval period (from which period a bath-house and Abbey church remain) and, especially, in the eighteenth and nineteenth centuries. It is the architecture of the eighteenth century that dominates Bath today.

Durham Cathedral and Castle

The Cathedral of Christ and the Blessed Virgin Mary stands on the site of an earlier church built to house the remains of the Saxon saint, Cuthbert. The old church, which by the time of its destruction also housed the bones of the Venerable Bede, usually known as the first English historian, was torn down and the present cathedral begun in 1093, essentially as a statement of power by the new Norman rulers. The present cathedral, whilst retaining much of its original Norman architecture, also includes some of the earliest examples of architectural features that are distinctively English in design. These include the ribbed vaulting of the choir aisles and the decorations on some of the pillars. The original central Norman tower was struck by lightening in 1429 and the resulting fire destroyed a copper-plated spire that had been added to it. The whole incident was related in writing by the Prior to the Bishop who was, presumably, away from Durham at the time:

'Most reverend and distinguished lord,...in the night before Corpus Christi, from ten o'clock even unto the seventh hour after midnight, there were in our parts horrible and unheard of thunderings and lightnings; and especially at the first hour after midnight such was the violence of the thunder when we were at Matins that we feared a great part of the church had fallen.
At this time the higher part of the great bell tower, by a flash of lightening, was put on fire.
...the fire lasted horribly, and the cupola of copper, being most intensely heated, fell down upon the church, but, blessed be the Highest, in a place not very harmful.'

The tombs of Bede and Cuthbert can still be seen in the cathedral.

The World Heritage site also includes a number of associated monastic buildings including a library, cloister and other chapels.

The original castle at Durham was built by the Normans in 1072 on the direct instructions of King William I. Parts of this building survive today, including the

Durham Cathedral and Castle.

Durham County Council

chapel, part of the keep and some of the curtain walling but the castle has been much extended and altered over the succeeding centuries. It was originally built as a fortified residence for the Bishop of Durham who, as the king's representative in the region, combined religious and military authority. However, as the Norman succession became accepted, the threat was from Scotland and the castle we see today has more to do with the protection of England than the imposition of Norman rule. Particular features to note are the magnificent twelfth-century (Bishop's) palace buildings and the late thirteenth-century great hall. The keep itself was almost totally rebuilt in the fourteenth century and rebuilt again in the nineteenth century when the castle became part of Durham University.

The castle and cathedral sit next to each other on a high sandstone outcrop that is surrounded by a loop of the river Wear and which dominates a major crossing point of the river. Together they form one of the finest architectural groupings in Europe.

The City of Edinburgh

Edinburgh combines an original medieval town plan with the world's most extensive example of a Romantic Classical city. Its Old Town, a royal burgh since the twelfth century, stretches downhill from the castle rock along the Royal Mile to the royal palace of Holyrood. This steep slope, flanked by unusually tall tenement buildings, still retains its medieval character although many original houses were destroyed in the wars with the English. There are seven 'New Towns' in the city each constructed using the finest available stone in the late eighteenth and early nineteenth centuries. The first was built on a rectangular grid, the second introduced curves while the third features a diagonally-set square at its centre. Known as 'The Athens of the North' the city consolidated its claim to this title in laying out its fourth New Town around the classically inspired monuments of Calton Hill.

Hadrian's Wall

Hadrian's Wall and its associated features are the most complex and best preserved of all the frontier works of the Roman Empire. Constructed on the order of the Emperor Hadrian in AD 122, the Wall stretched from the Tyne to the Solway and was extended down the Cumbrian coast by a series of small coastal forts and watchtowers. Originally the Wall probably stood over three metres high. Every Roman mile there was a small fort (or milecastle) and between each pair of milecastles there were two turrets. By the end of the second century AD the majority of the Wall was built in stone. Running behind it was a massive ditch flanked on either side by a bank, now known as the Vallum, which probably marked the rear edge of the Wall zone itself. Placed along or near the Wall were sixteen larger forts with garrisons of between 500 and

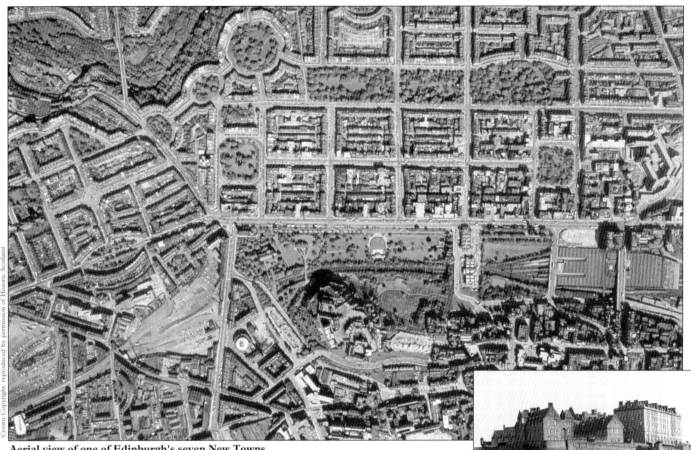

Aerial view of one of Edinburgh's seven New Towns.
Inset: Edinburgh Castle dominates the west end of the city.

1,000 men. Around these were civilian settlements and lying behind the Wall were the Roman towns of Carlisle and Corbridge. The approaches from the north were protected by outpost forts and the Wall itself was part of a system of military control based ultimately on the legionary fortresses at Chester and York.

The Wall was built across one of the narrowest parts of Britain where the main eastern and west-

ern communication routes to the north are linked by the relatively easy country of the Tyne Gap. The strategic importance of the area means that there are also many earlier Roman military works, such as marching camps and other more permanent bases, along the east-west Stanegate road. The road itself may have constituted an earlier control line before the decision was taken to build the Wall.

The remains survive remarkably well. Even in the most developed areas substantial remains are still visible, such as the forts at South Shields and Wallsend, and much more is known to remain buried. In east Northumberland, the Wall itself is largely

buried but the earthworks of its ditch and of the Vallum are visible for many miles and have had major effects on the post-Roman landscape. Associated features, such as the Roman town of Corbridge, are well preserved. In the central sector, the remains of the Wall and its associated features are prominent and often dominant in the local landscape. In this area too, other traces of Roman occupation such as the Stanegate road and its forts are well preserved as are some associated features such as marching camps. West of the central sector the archaeology is less obvious but still visible in places as earthworks and more frequently as buried deposits. Investigation has shown that remains survive even beneath urban Carlisle and down the Cumbrian coast at sites such as Maryport.

Hadrian's Wall at Cawfields milecastle showing the dramatic location of the wall on the left and the vallum on the right.

Stonehenge, Wiltshire, one of the most famous of all prehistoric monuments.

Stonehenge, Avebury and associated megalithic monuments

The sites included in this group designation include some of the most impressive prehistoric monuments in the world. The monuments at Avebury include the main circle that encompasses a village, a long stone alignment known as the West Kennet Avenue, the (in some cases partially) excavated sites of a number of other monuments, Silbury Hill (the largest artificial prehistoric mound in Northern Europe) and a large number of Neolithic and Bronze Age burial mounds. A number of the monuments were excavated and extensively restored in the earlier part of this century by the millionaire Alexander Keiller, who re-erected a number of stones that had either fallen or been deliberately buried in the medieval period – probably because of their perceived association with witchcraft and the devil. Other stones, both of the main circle and other monuments, were removed, mainly in the eighteenth century, for building material.

The landscape around Stonehenge is also full of prehistoric sites including the remains of two monuments comprising parallel earthen banks known as *Cursuses* and numerous Neolithic and Bronze Age burial mounds. Stonehenge itself, with its circle of worked sarsen (sandstone) stones capped by interlocking sarsen lintels that surrounds arrangements of smaller 'bluestones' (so called because of their colour and seem-

ingly transported over 200 miles specifically for use here) and five pairs of enormous worked sarsens each with their own capping stone, is unique.

Studley Royal Park including the ruins of Fountains Abbey

Originally laid out between 1716 and 1781 Studley Royal garden remains essentially unchanged and, as such, is one of the very few complete examples of an early formal eighteenth-century English garden. The site includes an earlier deer park, a number of artificial lakes, ponds and cascades as well as numerous statues, neo-classical temples and other garden monuments set within a wooded landscape. Within the boundaries of the site lie the ruins of the Cistercian Abbey of Fountains, founded in 1132. The Abbey was

dissolved and partially dismantled in AD 1539, along with most other monastic foundations in England, immediately following Henry VIII's disagreement with the Pope over the annulment of Henry's marriage to Catherine of Aragon in AD 1533. Its ruins stand as evidence of a period when the monasteries were a centre of considerable power and wealth – especially as they controlled much of the country's agricultural land.

The Tower of London

The first castle on this site was built under the orders of William the Conqueror immediately after the Norman invasion of 1066. However, most of the present buildings are of a later date. The White Tower, begun in 1079, was probably the first square (as opposed to the earlier circular) keep in the country. This building style was an ingenious innovation as it contained all of the necessary elements of earlier European palaces (impressive hall, chapel, service rooms and defences) within one extremely strong building: an obvious advantage for a minority and foreign elite. The castle has been added to extensively over the centuries and now covers 7.3ha (17.6 acres). The imposing curtain

The remains of the Cistercian Abbey of Fountains which now forms part of Studley Royal Park.

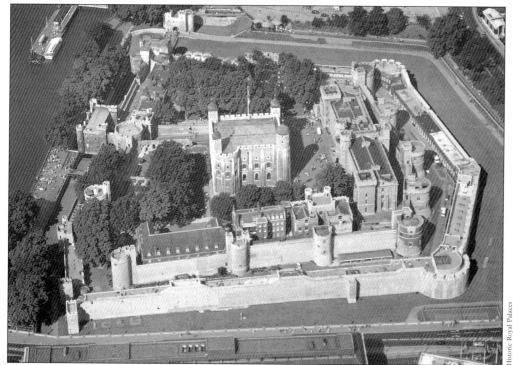

The Tower of London, first begun on the orders of William the Conqueror and added to and extended over the centuries.

late eleventh century and stands to the north of the Abbey. It is the official church for the House of Commons. The Palace is now renowned world-wide as a symbol of modern democratic government.

Ironbridge Gorge

The area along the River Severn (which includes the valleys of the two tributaries Coalbrooke and Hay Brook) contains some of the earliest examples of purpose-built industrial buildings associated with the Industrial Revolution. These include furnaces and smelters and a number of associated buildings and other features such as cottages, market squares and the remains of early railways. The world's first iron bridge was cast in Coalbrookedale by a local ironmaster, Abraham Darby, and erected

wall and associated 13 defensive towers of the inner bailey date mainly from the twelfth century. Military barracks were still being added in the nineteenth century.

The Tower has been a constant element in English history with countless famous prisoners held within its walls, many of whom left for execution through the infamous Traitor's Gate.

Part of Westminster Palace. Note the groups of tourists in the foreground all taking photographs of the buildings.

Westminster Palace and Abbey and St Margaret's Church

The Abbey church of Westminster was originally built by Edward the Confessor (1042–1066) but was extensively rebuilt by Henry III between 1245 and 1269. The present church includes some of the earliest and finest Early English and Decorated style architecture in the country. The Abbey church is particularly associated with the coronations of the British Royal Family.

The Palace of Westminster was originally built as one of the main royal residences. Two fires in 1512 and 1834 destroyed most of the medieval building with only Westminster Hall, the Jewel Tower and St Stephen's Cloister remaining from this period. The present complex mainly dates from the 1840–1867 re-building by the architect Sir Charles Barry and includes the chambers of the Houses of Lords and Commons (although the latter was redesigned by Sir Giles Gilbert Scott after being severely damaged by German bombing in 1941) and the tall clock tower famous for its 13 ton bell known as 'Big Ben'. St Margaret's church dates from the

The world's first iron bridge.

across the River Severn in 1779.

The area was one of the birthplaces of the Industrial Revolution. It was here that iron was first smelted with coke, and in the late eighteenth century it was probably the most important industrial centre in the world.

15

SOME OTHER WORLD HERITAGE SITES

MESA VERDE NATIONAL PARK, USA

For more than 2000 years the Ancestral Puebloan people of the American Southwest lived mainly as farmers in the Four Corners area of what is now Utah, Colorado, New Mexico, and Arizona. They grew corn, beans, and squash using dryland farming techniques. They traded with other communities as far west as the Gulf of California and south into Mexico, importing such items as cotton, turquoise, and shells. Noted for their skills in basket and pottery making, they developed distinctive designs which identify their wares. Originally, these people built pithouses on the mesa tops although they also used cliff alcoves for sleeping and shelter. Around AD 1200 the majority of people moved into the cliff alcoves, constructing the cliff dwellings for which the park is famous. Using sandstone blocks they chipped and shaped stones to use in the construction of these sites.

Although the earliest occupation of Mesa Verde dates to around AD 500, the cliff dwellings were only built during the final period from AD 1200–1300, and people lived in them for 100 years or less. During the late thirteenth century they began moving out of the area, heading south to the Rio Grande pueblos in New Mexico and the Hopi mesas in north-central Arizona. Reasons for leaving include drought, overuse of the land from extensive farming, a cooling period that may have shortened the growing season, and possibly even the emergence of new religious concepts to the south that drew them there. Descendants

Mesa Verde, Cliff Dwelling, 1950's reconstruction.

National Park Service

of these people still live today in the Rio Grande pueblos of New Mexico and the Hopi mesas of Arizona. Mesa Verde remained uninhabited until the late nineteenth century when miners, prospectors, and ranchers began exploring the area. Mesa Verde's over 4000 archaeological sites include 600 cliff dwellings, many mesa top pueblos, rock art panels, and small shrines. Cliff Palace, the largest cliff dwelling, has been excavated and stabilised, and receives about 170,000 visitors a year. It is closed during the winter months, but Spruce Tree House, the third largest cliff dwelling, remains open year round.

Current issues facing Mesa Verde National Park include overcrowding during the summer months, inadequate funds to stabilise and maintain the sites, air quality issues, and other sensitive topics such as the Native American

Graves Protection and Repatriation Act (NAGPRA). The NAGPRA Act includes provisions for discussions with Native American groups about artifacts taken out of the sites in the Park, especially those relating to human burials. Any skeletal remains may be reburied, and the grave goods may be returned to modern pueblo people. Overcrowding during the summer months causes parking problems as well as damage to the sites open to the public. In the future a reservation system may be necessary to control access to the park during the heavy summer travel months. Budget restrictions have curtailed the amount of stabilisation done to sites, leaving them open to further deterioration as time passes. All of these issues will affect the future of these fragile resources.

PETRA, JORDAN

The earliest settlement in Petra dates to 7,000 BC during the late Neolithic period but it was as the royal capital of the Nabataeans, a peaceful, Aramaic-speaking people who originally prospered by trading across the Arabian peninsula during the fourth century BC to the second century AD that it became famous. The city, as its name indicates, (in Greek 'Petra' literally means rock) was carved into, and out of, the rose-red coloured sandstone gorge in which it was concealed. Petra's unique blend of Classical and Oriental architecture set into a spectacular natural landscape make it one of the most beautiful World Heritage Sites.

The earliest known historical record of Petra is by Diodorus who gave an account of an unsuccessful attack in 312 BC by a former general of Alexander the Great. His objective was to loot the city which was known to be very rich from trade in frankincense, myrrh, spices and silver transported overland from southern Arabia. It may have been from this siege that the desert stronghold adopted its name.

While Diodorus portrays the inhabitants of Petra as an enterprising nomadic people, Strabo writing only a few decades later, sees them being totally urbanised. He describes Petra as a bustling international metropolis whose citizens enjoyed peace and prosperity. They lived in luxurious stone-built houses, kept numerous flocks and maintained sophisticated agricultural fields fed by complex irrigation systems.

Although heavily influenced by Greco-Roman traditions, Petra remained politically independent until AD 106 when it succumbed to Roman rule and became part of the Province of Arabia. In AD 130 the Roman Emperor Hadrian visited Petra and renamed it Petra Hadriane. Commerce flourished and it grew into a classical city complete with its theatres, nymphaeum, and colonnaded street.

In the fourth century during the Byzantine period, Petra was made the capital of Palestina Tertia and had a Christian population important enough to make it the seat of

The Obelisk Temple/Tomb, Petra, Jordan. Inset: Local people sell both fake artifacts and real objects excavated without permission to tourists eager to take a piece of the World Heritage home.

a bishop. Several churches were built, including a large basilica in the centre of the city. Monastic communities were also established, the most famous one at 'Aaron's Tomb'.

A series of earthquakes in the sixth century may have contributed to Petra's final demise, though it was more likely a combination of factors leading to the disruption of trade and general turmoil throughout Arabia by the seventh century. A period of abandonment and nomadic squatting ensued.

The crusaders built two castles in Petra during the twelfth century as a part of their south-eastern defence system extending from Jerusalem to Aqaba. After 1189 it returned to Arab control and served as a caravan stop on the routes through the Arabian peninsula. Medieval Arab travellers such as Ibn Batuta in the fourteenth century wrote of Petra's splendour, but it was not until 1812 when the Swiss explorer, Johanes Ludwig Burckhardt 're-discovered' it that the site became known in the West. During the nineteenth century a number of artists and writ-

ers, for example David Roberts and Edward Lear, visited Petra and the site inspired many works of art and literature. Most recently it was used in the final dramatic scene of the film 'Indiana Jones and the Temple of Doom'.

The natural aura of Petra has encouraged generations to dwell, build and thrive in this desert environment. However, the once isolated city is now faced with all of the problems of fleeting mass international tourism and today millions flock to visit this site.

Unfortunately, Petra's narrow entrance, known as the 'siq', and delicate sandstone buildings were never intended to accommodate such numbers. The Jordanian government is making attempts to protect the ancient site by forbidding mounted horses in the 'siq' and limiting commercial development. A cafe has also been placed in the site quite close to the entrance that encourages many visitors to stop for refreshments and then leave. In this way the rest of the site is protected from large numbers of visitors. The entrance fee to the site has also recently been raised, to the equivalent of £25.00, to deter casual visitors and to raise funds for the site's conservation. In addition to the sheer number of visitors the authorities are faced with the problem of local Bedouin excavating – or looting – archaeological areas to find artifacts to sell to tourists. It will only be when tourists refuse to buy such memorabilia of the visits that the finite archaeological resource will be safeguarded.

GREAT ZIMBABWE, ZIMBABWE

The ruins at Great Zimbabwe have become a symbol of not only free Zimbabwe but the whole of black Africa. Indeed, Zimbabwe actually took its name from this type of archaeological site which means 'houses of stone' or possibly ' venerated house'. The remains at Great Zimbabwe were constructed between AD 1100 and AD 1500. At its peak the site was a home to an estimated 12,000 to 17,000 people and it was the largest, and most powerful, sub-Saharan settlement prior to European colonisation. Its wealth was based on cattle, agriculture and the control of the trade routes between the gold fields in the north and the Indian ocean in the east. By the fifteenth century its dominance had begun to decline, probably mainly as the result of political changes and perhaps the over-exploitation of agricultural land, and it had been all but abandoned by the seventeenth century.

The site originally consisted of two types of structure: stone walls and clay buildings. The stone walls, which are all that is visible today, were built to screen and divide the space between the buildings which were residential homes. The site is also divided between the hill complex which, by tradition, would have been the residence of the king, and the valley-bottom settlement which would have been home for the majority of the population. Also on the valley floor is the Great Enclosure. The function of this magnificent enclosure is not entirely clear but it may be evidence of a move of royal power down from the hilltop to the valley floor. Another interpretation is that it was the home of one or more of the royal wives and another is that it was the site of a premarital initiation school. Whatever its function this building emphasises the enormous skill of the builders with parallel dry stone walls soaring up to ten metres in height. Inside the Great Enclosure is a massive, solid conical tower the function of which is again unclear. It has been suggested that it represents a grain bin as the pro-

tection of the harvest was one of the main responsibilities of the king.

Despite the evidence provided by archaeologists, it was not until very recently that it was accepted more widely that the remains at Great Zimbabwe were the work of an indigenous population. As part of

This early reconstruction (above) of the main entrance into the Great Enclosure, has been dismantled and rebuilt along more likely lines (right).

the justification for white colonial domination was that the whites had introduced civilization to the area it was impossible for the ruling minority to accept that a powerful, indigenous society had flourished in the area long before white colonisation. Numerous explanations were put forward including that the site had been built by the Queen of Sheba, the Phoenicians, Arab traders and the Portuguese. Some of the early restoration work at the site carried out in the early part of this century, at one of the main entrances to the Great Enclosure, was explicitly based on a Middle Eastern architectural style to re-enforce the supposed link with the Queen of Sheba. Such overtly racist interpretations were slowly, but eventually totally, dismantled by archaeologists working from the results of scientific excavations and the incorrect reconstruction has now been dismantled and rebuilt in a style that reflects the original

remains on site. However, this was not achieved without sacrifice and the Head of the Monuments Commission was forced to resign in the early 1970s following political pressure to conceal the evidence for the indigenous pedigree of the site.

The main conservation problems at Great Zimbabwe are concerned with the dry stone walls. Many have stood for over eight hundred years but are increasingly susceptible to deterioration caused both by simple attrition or more dramatic collapse – especially during spells of heavy rainfall. The quite dramatic growth in the number of tourists visiting the site has significantly increased the attritional damage by visitors wearing out cir-

culation routes and climbing on the walls and inadvertently dislodging loose stones. Others have been seen to remove stones for souvenirs. Another problem is that baboons dislodge stones from the tops of walls while searching for scorpions that are sheltering in the stones to eat. An early conservation report suggested the removal of the baboons from the site. However, baboons and all of the flora and fauna of the area, attract foreign visitors and it is the tourist dollar that helps to fund conservation work. Overall however, tourists and baboons are thought to cause only superficial damage. Most wall collapses are caused by structural instabilities which only become acute problems over long periods of time. The National Museums and Monuments of Zimbabwe has now established, with international support, a major conservation programme at the site.

ULURU-KATA TJUTA NATIONAL PARK, AUSTRALIA

This site, probably better known to most people in the west as Ayers Rock, was inscribed on the World Heritage List as a natural property in 1987. The site was nominated because of its rare and scientifically important flora and fauna and for its unique geology. However, in 1994, the Park was re-inscribed on the List as the second example of a Cultural Landscape (see page 6).

The Park is situated on traditional Aboriginal lands where Aboriginal people still live and where Aboriginal languages are still spoken extensively as the first language. Ownership of the land was formally returned by the Australian Government to local Aboriginal people, the Anangu, in 1985 in a ceremony now referred to as 'handback'. The Anangu immediately leased the National Park back to the Australian Nature Conservation Agency (ANCA) and both groups now jointly manage the site through a Board of six Anangu and four non Anangu representatives. The management of the site is guided primarily by Anangu law and tradition – *Tjukurpa* – thus emphasising the right of Aboriginal peoples to be the main custodians of their traditional lands and the importance of Uluru-Kata Tjuta as an important cultural landscape. The 1994 renomination documentation, which was prepared in full co-operation with Anangu people, argued that the site was an 'associative cultural landscape' as it has powerful religious, artistic and cultural associations for Anangu people with an active social and spiritual role in contemporary society, and that it was a 'continuing cultural landscape' since it is managed by the Anangu using the Aboriginal techniques of selective burning which have been practised for over 20,000 years.

One of the first decisions taken by the new management Board was to remove a number of tourist facilities, including an airstrip and several modern roads, that had grown up very close to the site and to replace them with new facilities at a more respectful distance from the site and from the local Anangu community. In 1995, ten years after handback, a Cultural Centre was opened at the site. The Centre is made up of two low profile snake-like buildings the design of which reflect two of the ancestral beings important to the Anangu; Aboriginal designers and craftsmen worked on the complex. The site for the Centre was originally identified by local elders and agreed upon after surveys were carried out to ensure that no rare flora or fauna would be endangered. The Centre and associated car parks have been carefully landscaped to protect and blend with the environment and its courtyard has a spectacular view towards Uluru.

The management strategy of the site, including the interpretation and commercial enterprises at the Cultural Centre, sets out to enable the Anangu to present visitors with information concerning their culture, knowledge and traditional land management policies as enshrined in the *Tjukurpa*. This policy of presenting the site as it is – a living part of Anangu spiritual life – has been put into practice in other ways in the management of the site, for example, some important sacred sites now have restricted access while photography is restricted at others. The strategy also supports the local community through training Anangu people to work as Rangers and Guides, in the administration and management of the site, and by providing an outlet for local crafts and art.

The developments at Uluru-Kata Tjuta represent a huge step forward in the move towards bridging a gulf between people with immensely differing cultural values and perceptions. It is hoped that the lessons learnt here can be transferred elsewhere and that visitors continue to develop a fuller appreciation of, and a greater sensitivity towards, the culture of their hosts.

'NGANANA TATINTJA WIYA' – WE DON'T CLIMB

Traditional owners of Uluru prefer that visitors do not climb the rock.

What visitors call 'the climb' is the traditional route taken by ancestral Mala men on their arrival at Uluru and the path is of spiritual significance.

When we leased the Park to the Australian National Parks and Wildlife Service, we agreed to continue to allow people to climb the rock at a designated place. This saddens our people, as we do not regard climbing the rock as being lawful or right.

As well, Traditional Owners have a duty to safeguard visitors on their land. Anangu feel a great sadness when a person dies or is hurt on the climb.

Through the Park's management, we have tried to explain our feelings over this, and have encouraged people 'not to climb'.

An increasing number of visitors have recognised the existence of our Law, and do not climb.'

Text from a Uluru-Kata Tjuta National Park leaflet.

'Yet 80% of the 1000 people who visit the rock each day faithfully make the long trek up'.
The Weekend Australian, 20–21 January 1996.

Despite the pleas of local peoples most tourists still insist on climbing Uluru.

DUBROVNIK, CROATIA

By the thirteenth century this tiny town nestling on the Croatian coast was one of the most successful trading centres of the known world. Its position on the Adriatic coast between the economic and cultural traditions of East and West made it an obvious centre for economic and cultural exchange. Because of its size, position and wealth the city was always under threat of attack from a succession of potential aggressors but it was consistently protected by others who saw the advantage of having such a free centre for trade and exchange.

The walled city covers an area of only 15.2ha (36.6 acres) and the World Heritage listing includes all the buildings within the walled area. Apart from its architectural splendour, Dubrovnik is also important because it has a wealth of documentary information concerning its original building and its reconstruction after a devastating earthquake in 1667. As such the city presents an almost complete record of medieval urban planning and development.

By the end of the eighteenth century Dubrovnik's role as an economic centre was beginning to be usurped by others and the city became a backwater with its population becoming dependent on local industries – especially fishing. In recent years Dubrovnik has become almost totally reliant upon its tourist industry.

Sadly Dubrovnik's peaceful existence as a tourist destination was shattered in the early 1990s when the former Yugoslavia collapsed into war. As a World Heritage Site Dubrovnik should have enjoyed the protection not only of the 1972 UNESCO *Convention concerning the protection of the World Cultural and Natural Heritage* but also of the 1954 UNESCO *Convention for the Protection of Cultural Property in the Event of Armed Conflict* (The Hague Convention). Unfortunately little notice has been taken by any side in the conflict of these Conventions and in 1991 and again in May and June 1992 the city was the target for heavy and

The old city of Dubrovnik was especially targeted during the fighting in the former Yugoslavia as a cultural emblem of Croatia.

The main street in the old city before the war bustling with tourists. Tourism is slowly returning.

UNESCO

Jasenka Zovela-Spivalo

deliberate shelling from land, sea and air as the aggressors seemingly attempted the systematic destruction of what they perceived of as an emblem of Croatian sovereignty. As soon as the attacks on the city began, appeals to stop the destruction were made by Dr Federico Mayor, Director-General of UNESCO and by a host of other cultural organisations throughout the world. The city was put on the World Heritage in Danger List in December 1991. Damage was extensive but as soon as hostilities ceased a UNESCO-organised international team moved in to help local experts assess the damage and plan for the conservation and restoration of the city. The initial survey noted that 563, 68%, of buildings had been

damaged. Fires resulting from the barrage had completely destroyed nine buildings.

A complete Plan of Action has now been formalised and set into motion and tourists are beginning to return to the city. Much of the city has been restored but much still needs to be done.

'In a cultural war, the conquest of territories and the "ethnic cleansing" of settlements is insufficient. Nothing less than the destruction of past historical identities is needed. If the identities between past nations and their landscapes are best symbolised by their monuments, it is these monuments which have been prime targets in this cultural war. Mosques for Serbs and Croats, Orthodox churches for Muslims and Croats, Catholic monasteries for Serbs and Muslims – each monumental symbol fatally attracts the cultural warriors. Designation of a building for UNESCO Protection marks out buildings for special destruction. Even the reduction of standing monuments to rubble may not be sufficient: Povrzanovi, writing in 1993, refers to instances in newly-conquered Serbian territory where even ruined Catholic churches are an affront to Serbian settlers.'

John Chapman, *Antiquity* 1994

THE ATHENIAN ACROPOLIS, GREECE

The Athenian Acropolis houses four of the masterpieces of Greek architecture: the Propylaea or gate house to the Acropolis; the Parthenon, a temple to the goddess Athena; the Erechtheion, an Ionic style building with the *Caryatids*, sculptured figures used as structural columns; and the Temple of Athena Nike.

The centrepiece of the Acropolis is the Parthenon, which is frequently described as the epitome of Greek architecture. It was commissioned by Pericles in the fifth century BC as the setting for a colossal statue of Athena and as a secure treasury for the funds of the Greek Confederacy. More recently the building was used as a Christian church and later as a Muslim mosque. In 1687 when Greece was occupied by the Turks, the Acropolis was besieged by the Venetians. The Parthenon was being used as an ammunition store and a stray Venetian shell caused a huge explosion that resulted in a great deal of damage. Since then the building has been a ruin. In 1801 Lord Elgin, who at the time was British Ambassador to the Ottoman Empire, obtained permission from the occupying Turkish forces to remove a number of pieces of sculpture from the Parthenon. His agents almost certainly overreached their authority by actually removing substantial parts of the frieze and other decorative elements from the building itself. These so-called 'Elgin Marbles' are now housed in the British Museum.

The buildings on the Acropolis have been exposed to natural decay as the result of rain, hail, wind and especially frost for nearly two and a half thousand years. Recently these natural problems have been substantially multiplied by the effects of human action. The atmospheric pollution that stems from Athens being a major centre of population and industry is proving to have potentially catastrophic implications for the Acropolis buildings. The main causes of damage are the sulphur and nitrogen compounds contained in industrial and domestic central heating fumes and the nitrogen produced from car exhausts. When combined with any humidity these gases are converted into acids, which attack the surface of the marble. Some of the resulting products attract other dirt pollution and form a crust over the marble which eventually cracks the surface of the stone. As a direct result of this damage, the Greek government is taking a number of measures to reduce the general level of pollution in the city, including the banning of motor vehicles from the immediate environs of the Acropolis, and is introducing a longer-term plan to replace a particular type of heating oil as the main fuel for central heating.

A second problem has been directly caused by restoration work that was carried out between 1896 and 1933. The ancient Greeks used small iron bolts to hold some stones together but made them almost rust proof by coating them with lead. Unfortunately, these were replaced, during the restoration work, with steel bolts that have rusted badly because of the high humidity and proximity to the sea. This has not only weakened the buildings but has also caused the steel to swell and crack the marble that it is supposedly securing. Over the last twenty years a programme has been underway to replace all of the steel with titanium – a metal that should not rust.

A third major threat is the number of tourists who wish to visit the site. Visitor numbers have risen to the point where they are actually eroding the monument at a visible rate. In 1995 over a million people paid to visit the Acropolis, a figure that does not include many thousands of educational visitors, and others, who were allowed free access. All visitors now pass through passages especially designed for pedestrians which have been constructed as part of the restoration and preservation project. Wooden steps have also been erected over the marble steps of the Propylaea to prevent further erosion by visitors' feet.

Finally the Acropolis raises the issue of the return of cultural property. The 'Elgin Marbles' are the largest but by no means only group of sculptures belonging to the site that are now housed in major museums around the world. Their removal has certainly kept them in a far better state of preservation than most, if not all, of the sculpture that was not removed. However, the Greek government has formally requested the return of the Elgin Marbles on a number of occasions, so that they may be housed in a purpose built museum in Athens. These requests have been met by the response that they were removed legally in the nineteenth century and that their return would need an Act of the British Parliament to release them from the British Museum. The controversy goes on.

Tamara Corbishley

The Parthenon.

CULTURAL TOURISM: BENEFITS AND PROBLEMS

■ In the 1993 survey of Overseas Visitors to London, 37% of visitors quote heritage as being of particular importance.

■ In 1993 the English Tourist Board estimated that 33% of visitors to historic buildings that year were from overseas. This compares with 26% for museums and art galleries, 13% for gardens and 3% for wildlife attractions.

BENEFITS

Tourism is one of the United Kingdom's most important industries both economically, as it makes a major direct contribution to the economy, and socially, as it employs large numbers of people who, in turn, have spare money to spend on leisure and tourism. In 1995 tourism spending in the UK amounted to £36.6 billion (£12.4 billion from overseas visitors, £14.4 billion from domestic tourists' overnight trips, £9.7 billion from domestic day trips). These figures accounted for 4.0% of the UK's Gross Domestic Product (rising to 4.5% when day trips are included) and for 6.3% of total consumer spending (around 10% with day trips).

Tourism and heritage are mutually interdependent and surveys consistently show that heritage is one of the main reasons for overseas visitors choosing the UK as a holiday destination. There were 66.7 million visits to historic attractions in 1994 which represents approximately 20% of the total number of visits to all attractions. Over 10 million people annually visit the UK sites on the World Heritage List. Together

with the countryside, culture and heritage stimulate approximately 66% of visits made by foreign tourists. It is estimated that each year 40% of UK residents visit at least one historic building during the peak season. A growth rate of 17.7% on these figures is forecast between 1994–1999.

PROBLEMS

Unfortunately, large numbers of visitors can have a detrimental effect on the places they are visiting especially if, as is usually the case with cultural sites, the ambience of the site is part of why people wish to visit. Some sites suffer from problems of access, with congested approach roads and overcrowded car parks, as used to be the case at Fountains Abbey (see page 25). Others, for example, Westminster Abbey, suffer from overcrowding on site with visitors congregating around what they perceive to be the most important or attractive part(s) of the site. Some sites are literally being worn away by visitors' feet, as at

The provision of an interpretation panel at Avebury resulted in this whole area being turned into a muddy quagmire by tourists eager to read the information on the panel.

Peter Stone

Avebury where paths have been worn into the bank of the monument. Overcrowding can also spoil the atmosphere of a site, as was happening at Canterbury Cathedral.

CASE STUDY: CANTERBURY CATHEDRAL

Of the three parts of this World Heritage Site (see page 10) only the Cathedral attracts enough visitors to cause problems in tourist management. The Cathedral receives upwards of two million visitors in a year making it the most popular tourist attraction in South East England outside London.

Along with many other sites the Cathedral experienced a huge increase in visitor numbers in the late 1970s as the tourist industry developed quickly. Until then the management of visitors was carried out largely by dedicated but, amateur volunteers organised by one secretary with a diary and pencil. Provision was made for guided tours, and there were guide books available and interpretation notices in various parts of the building, but, aside from this, little else was done for the visitor. At the beginning of the 1980s, the Dean and Chapter were becoming so concerned by the numbers of visitors that a completely fresh approach was taken.

Unlike many other sites, concern is not primarily with the physical erosion of the fabric. It has always been the tradition, enshrined in the Rule of St Benedict, to welcome all comers to the Cathedral and if that means the replacement of, for example, floors, from time to time, then this is something that the

Dean and Chapter are ready to accept. Obviously, treasures such as the Black Prince's Achievements or the Wall Paintings in St Gabriel's Chapel are given special protection but the overall philosophy is that the Cathedral is there to be used. The main concern was that the huge number of visitors, by the very fact of their number, were not enjoying a meaningful experience and were preventing others from so doing.

In 1983 a Canon with specific responsibility to tackle this problem was appointed. It was not an easy task to undertake, requiring, as it did, the redefinition of functions and responsibilities performed by volunteers who had been working there for many years. It needed the imposition of a more rigid management system and the introduction of professional standards of visitor care. By 1986 the new organisation was ready and the first lay Director of Visits was appointed.

Under the new system two new categories of visitor carers have been created, the *Welcomer* and the *Assistant*, both with distinctive uniforms. *Welcomers*, who are paid a small retainer, stand at the west end of the Cathedral, close to the door by which the majority of visitors enter, to greet them and hand out a free leaflet. This leaflet is now printed in nine different languages. *Welcomers* originally stood next to the voluntary donation boxes and the mere presence of staff in that spot led to an immediate and quite significant increase in income, to the extent that the extra costs of the new measures were more than adequately covered. *Assistants*, of whom as many as six can be on duty at any one time, are positioned inside the Cathedral at strategic points, primarily to assist the visitor. They do have other duties, such as ensuring reasonable behaviour and, on very busy days, human traffic control, but their first priority is that of care.

At managerial level, the Director of Visitors is in charge of the day to day running of the new Visits' Department and the Education Centre. This means that volunteers can be more logically and economically organised. An audio visual presentation and audio tours have been introduced giving the visitor a much wider choice in gaining an interpretation of the building and its meaning.

By 1990 these measures were working well but there was one remaining problem. The proximity of Canterbury to the mainland of Europe means that continental school parties come in large numbers. The discipline of these groups was frequently poor and it

Canterbury Cathedral, discipline of foreign groups was often poor until the Shepherd system was introduced.

Dean and Chapter of Canterbury

was commonplace for groups of children to be left in the Cathedral Precincts, which are safe and relatively traffic free, whilst the supervising adults went off to shop in the town. The result was that bored youngsters would roam in the Cathedral, learning nothing and disturbing other visitors as well as endangering the Cathedral's function as a place of worship. To deal with this problem discussions were held in both Paris and Lille with representatives of the education authorities and travel agents who bring these groups to Canterbury and a management system was introduced known as Operation Shepherd. A team of mainly young people, has been recruited and are known as *Shepherds*. The *Shepherds* wear a distinctive uniform and an area

just outside the main entrance into the Cathedral has been designated as a waiting area for school groups. There they are divided into parties of no more than twenty and one of their adult supervisors is put in charge wearing a badge on which is written the name of the school. Entry into the Cathedral is phased as and when there is enough space inside without causing congestion. Each leader is given a leaflet in an appropriate language explaining the route to be followed and the main features of the Cathedral to make the visit more meaningful.

In June 1995 an entrance charge to the Precincts was introduced. This was a purely financial measure as projected losses were £500,000 each year to the end of the century and beyond. The voluntary donation system was producing just 12.4 pence per visitor. By choosing the Precincts rather than the Cathedral as the payment point it has been possible to improve visitor management and to partially restore the peaceful ambience which had been in danger of disappearing. The charge is not implemented at times when formal services are taking place, thus preserving the overriding consideration of the Cathedral as a place of worship.

DISCUSSION POINTS: TOURISM

Students could use the information in this book and other published material to research the measures taken at various sites to cope with visitors. As all of the examples in the book show, the management of sites is complex and multi-faceted with the management of visitors being inextricably linked to the

This special protective pathway is being tested at Stonehenge in order to protect the delicate archaeology and to allow visitors to walk all around the main circle.

English Heritage Photo Library

protection and conservation of sites. Some sites produce materials for students that may deal with tourism and management issues (see Bibliography and resources) and most will answer written requests for information. Some students may wish to interview managers of sites – but **please remember** that staff are usually extremely busy and cannot deal with too many requests for personal interviews.

Visitor surveys

With the permission of site managers, students could produce questionnaires and conduct a survey of visitors. If the questionnaires are devised in conjunction with site managers the work may actually be of real benefit to the site. Topics for discussion might include:

■ Whether the history of the site makes it of particular relevance to local/regional/national/world tourism?

■ Do tourists from different locations come to visit the site for different reasons?

■ Has the site been a tourist destination for a long time? Why/why not?

Conservation and profit

Students could also study the economic aspects of site management: could revenue be increased, and if so how? If increased, should the extra funding go solely to the conservation of the site or to promoting other aspects of the tourist infrastructure? Many tourists (especially wealthy ones) will not visit areas or sites with poor facilities, but if money is not spent on preserving and conserving the monuments there will soon nothing for tourists to visit. Which element of this equation do students think is most important? The economics of conservation vary considerably depending on where you are in the world. For example, some countries may be able to spend the same amount on merely advertising their site or sites as other, less wealthy, countries are

able to spend on conserving their site or sites. Should the international community do something more about helping those countries conserve sites that cannot afford it? If so, what? and how?

The visitor is the most important person

The British Tourist Authority recently published *Guidelines for Tourism 1993/97*. This listed the strengths of the British tourism product and set out a range of matters to be addressed:

■ the need to maintain the quality of the environment and for tourist attractions to be sustainable and sensitive to the needs of the host community

■ the need to expand the season and to spread the load of tourism

■ the need to improve the quality and level of provision of information and interpretation

■ the need to provide materials in foreign languages and to encourage the speaking of languages by staff

■ the need to make provision for disabled people at tourist attractions

■ the need for enhanced provision of customer care training.

Students could look at these issues with respect to one or more sites they visit. How much further work do they think that site managers need to do before the Tourist Board Guidelines will be met? More generally, the BTA appears to assume that the visitor is always the most important element of any visit. Students could discuss this – especially in relation to the management of sites such as Uluru (see page 19).

One of the paintings at Lascaux.

Limiting site facilities can be used as a means of visitor management. If a particular site already receives so many visitors that they are becoming a threat to its long-term preservation, a reduction in facilities may actually deter some visitors. Such a strategy could be coupled by an increase in facilities at a nearby site with spare visitor capacity, or by the removal of the first site's facilities to a location some distance from the actual site. In the latter case the facility can actually take on the function of a 'surrogate' attraction with visitors learning about the real site without ever actually visiting it. In an extreme version of this approach, managers of the World Heritage Site of Lascaux in France took the unprecedented step, in 1963, of actually closing the site to visitors in order to protect the 20,000 year old art from bacteria and algae introduced by those visiting the cave. Today, only five bona fide scientists are allowed into the cave on five days out of seven and this only for a

short time. However, the authorities were aware of vast numbers of people still wanting to see the art and therefore decided to create an artificial cave close to the real one with the art replicated on its, authentic looking, concrete walls. Visitors still flock to Lascaux II as the replica cave is known to see the reproduction art and to learn about the conservation problems facing the real cave. A similar solution to the problems of visitor erosion has been suggested for Stonehenge but the idea of constructing a full-scale replica monument, some distance away from the real one, has been rejected.

THE NEED FOR VISITOR FACILITIES

The World Heritage Site Operational Guidelines emphasise the need for World Heritage Sites to be an integral part of their landscape and for their setting not to be spoilt by unnecessary or unsuitable development (see pages 29 to 31 and Bibliography and resources). However, if tourists are going to visit cultural sites some provision needs to be made for facilities for them. The type and quality of any such facilities will need to be carefully researched, discussed and planned as their provision may have a direct affect on the conservation and ambience of a site and will almost certainly require a significant financial commitment. The provision of facilities will also need to take into account existing provision within the local area and should be an integral part of local or regional tourist plans. At some sites provision may only need to be very basic as suitable facilities will already exist nearby. More remote sites may need the full range of facilities – including overnight accommodation.

UNESCO now expects States Parties to provide appropriate facilities at World Heritage sites and, where facilities do not exist, for these to be part of the proposed development strategy within the site's management plan. UNESCO encourages site managers to position any new building development outside the area designated as the World Heritage Site and to ensure that any new building is designed to be as unobtrusive as possible.

Unfortunately, a number of sites have already been affected by unsuitable development and it is now the task of the managers of these sites to attempt to redress the balance and, if possible, remove or at least lessen the impact of such development.

CASE STUDY: FOUNTAINS ABBEY AND STUDLEY ROYAL – VISITOR CENTRE

The National Trust acquired this site in 1983 and immediately embarked upon a long term programme of restoration and conservation of the whole property, much of which was in very poor repair. The site consists of three main parts: the Abbey ruins, the gardens and the deer park (see page 14).

The Trust inherited limited visitor facilities situated at the heart of the site in locations that were both archaeologically sensitive and historically important. The facilities,

The old visitor facilities at Studley Royal – queues were a common problem.

which had grown-up over the years in an unplanned and piecemeal manner, were inadequate, unsightly and intrusive. Indeed, the whole visitor experience was negative from before people even arrived at the site as the narrow approach roads and local villages were frequently heavily congested with cars and coaches attempting to reach the estate. Once visitors had braved the traffic queues they had to fight for space in bleak car parks that often overflowed onto archaeologically sensitive land adjacent to the Abbey. There was little opportunity to provide visitors with appropriate information

or interpretation because of the lack of suitable buildings. The peace, tranquillity and beauty of the site were marred by queuing at ticket offices and cafe kiosks, and by overcrowding in the area around the Abbey caused by the sheer pressure of visitors, who were often unaware of the existence of other parts of the estate or felt that they were too remote.

The Trust therefore decided that a new visitor centre was required that would enable it to

■ remove eyesores and improve other existing inadequate facilities

■ locate more centrally and greatly improve visitor facilities, information and interpretation for all, including disabled visitors

■ manage visitors in a more effective way thereby enhancing the visitor experience

■ encourage more visitors to see the whole of the site thereby spreading the visitor load across the site and reducing wear on the most popular areas

■ cater for an increasing number of visitors target new categories of visitors including foreign tourists, coach parties, family groups, visitors with special needs and educational visitors

■ increase the revenue from visitors.

This last aim was fundamental to the whole project as it tied the management of visitors into the much wider programme for restoration and preservation. The restoration programme relies almost entirely on revenue produced by the site and it was the Trust's belief that revenue could only be increased if visitors were provided with a comfortable,

The new visitor facilities blend traditional building techniques with modern visitor needs.

interesting and enjoyable experience.

The Trust identified a number of possible locations for new visitor facilities but decided for a variety of reasons that all but one were unsuitable: some would merely perpetuate the existing problems; others would introduce unwelcome buildings into inappropriate areas of the site; while most had the disadvantage of intruding on the ambience of the site and threatening its long-term conservation. The Trust therefore decided to construct new facilities on an adjacent farm which had recently been bought as a buffer zone to protect the Abbey site. A scheme was eventually approved by the Local Planning Authority in 1991. The facilities include a landscaped car park and purpose-designed building on a new site hidden from the Abbey, gardens and park, linked to a main road by a new access road built on land specially purchased by the Trust for that purpose. 30,000 trees and shrubs and a mile of new hedgerow have been planted to screen the facilities, to increase wildlife habitats and to create attractive wooded areas for visitors to enjoy. The new, single story, building houses information and interpretation facilities alongside lavatories, cafe and shop.

The design of the new visitor facilities is purposely modern with a visible steel structure, although it is clad in local traditional materials.

In this way the Trust believes that it is extending the tradition of new building on the site, that has continued since the Abbey was first constructed, while at the same time ensuring it sits comfortably in the landscape. The facilities have been designed to cope with at least 350,000 visitors a year, effectively extending the upper limit on visitor numbers which had been reached in 1991. Their position, within convenient walking distance of the Abbey, gardens and Park, has encouraged visitors to follow circular routes, rather than returning in their own tracks as most did

previously. This has greatly reduced visitor pressure, and is safeguarding the fabric and atmosphere of the Abbey ruins. The all-weather facilities have also encouraged visiting in the spring, autumn and winter, when the estate is particularly beautiful, thus helping to spread visitor numbers over the full twelve months. The increased revenue from the new facilities is assisting the Trust to continue with the restoration programme and to achieve its long term objectives set out in the management plan currently being finalised.

Not everyone agrees with the use of visitor centres to provide the necessary interpretation or facilities for tourists. Here two individuals lament their use:

'...as the 1970s showed, nothing dates more quickly than a visitor centre. The all time horror is the hideous example at Furness Abbey in Cumbria. It looks like a Post Office sorting depot. At Conisbrough in Yorkshire a theme-park style space capsule blocks the view of the castle as you walk through the gate...Interpretation – explaining the history of a monument – is ephemeral; attitudes towards interpretation change constantly. That is why it should not be enshrined in new permanent structures.'

Marcus Binney, *The Times* 5 June 1996

'At Fountains Abbey, most regrettably, the new visitors' centre has to be described as exploitation in its own right: its whole scale and character seem aimed at rivalling the Abbey ruins and wiping them out of one's mind as one returns to leave the site through the visitors' centre. Its huge cost is reflected in high entrance prices that visitors so strongly resent. "Isn't this our monument?", they write, again and again in the comments book. "We cannot afford to come again". '

Lord Kennet, speaking in a House of Lords debate on World Heritage Sites on 21 October 1993.

CASE STUDY: STONEHENGE

At Stonehenge rather ugly, and now totally inadequate, visitor facilities had also grown up too close to the stone circle. There are also two major trunk roads which pass within a few hundreds metres of the circle cutting it off from the surrounding landscape, and the prehistoric remains it holds, which is part of the designated World Heritage Site.

Visitor facilities and access

In the 1960s visitor numbers to Stonehenge rose to over 300,000 annually. To help provide a safer and more enjoyable visit the present underpass was built, the car park was increased in size and toilets, souvenir and refreshment facilities improved. The present facilities, which now have to cope with over 700,000 paying visitors a year, are mainly housed within these 1960s buildings and there-

The present visitor facilities become extremely overcrowded and cannot cope with numbers wishing to visit - especially in the summer.

fore, unfortunately, visitors do not have as enjoyable or educational a visit as they might otherwise have if there was space for suitable facilities.

Also, despite a variety of interpretation techniques, most visitors regard the site to consist solely of the stone circle and ignore the countless other prehistoric monuments in the surrounding landscape. With the increasing number of visitors, the grass inside the stone circle became a muddy

quagmire every time it rained and gravel was laid down to protect the remaining below-ground archaeology and to provide a less messy surface. However, the gravel stuck to people's shoes and began to damage the stones as they scrambled all over them. Therefore, in 1978, the site was returned to grass and visitor access to the centre circle restricted. Most visitors are therefore constrained to following a pathway that goes around the main circle and then leave without appreciating even the existence of other prehistoric remains in the area.

The actual centre circle at Stonehenge is closed to visitors, reducing direct erosion and allowing visitors the chance to take photographs unspoilt by other visitors.

Roads

Just to the north of the circle the A344 passes within metres of one of the outlying stones and actually bisects the neolithic monument known as the Avenue. Paying visitors have to pass under this road through the 1960s concrete underpass to reach the site from the car park. Many visitors decide not to pay and, quite literally, dice with death by crossing the road at a blind spot for drivers who are frequently speeding. A few hundred metres to the south lies the A303 – one of the main routes from London to the South West. The section of this road that passes Stonehenge is one of the last sections of the whole route not to be upgraded into dual carriageway. The

'I wonder whether the officials devising the routes were aware that the Department of Transport is just as much bound by the 1972 Convention as is any other part of the Government. For that part of the A303, the only thing that can make sense is a long tunnel from east of King Barrow Hill to west of Long Barrow roundabout. That, I hope, is what English Heritage and the National Trust have told the Department of Transport. It will of course be expensive, but that is something upon which they cannot scrimp. This is one of the very oldest and grandest things in the world. The cost of tunnelling is coming down all the time. The Department of Transport is spending, it says, £1,509 million on new construction this year and next, which is 64% of its total expenditure. The rest relates to the improvement of older roads. So the money is there – it really is – if the priorities can be got right.'

Lord Kennet, speaking in a House of Lords debate on World Heritage Sites on 21 October 1993.

Department of Transport has discussed a number of options for the upgrading including moving the road to routes well to the north or south of the present line of the road, widening the road along the present line in a deep cutting, or putting lengths of the road into a tunnel.

Everyone concerned with the management of Stonehenge is convinced that the visitor facilities and all other twentieth-century clutter should be removed and relocated outside the World Heritage Site in order for the main circle to be returned to a grassland environment, reunited with many of its associated prehistoric monuments and freed from the noise, damage and intrusion of the two trunk roads. In fact, quite a lot of development has already been removed, including a pig farm and military airfield that were both easily visible from the stone circle. For a number of years English Heritage

Projection Visual Communications

An illustration showing what Stonehenge looks like today and what it might look like if the A344 were to be closed and grassed over.

(which manages the area between the roads) and the National Trust (which owns much of the land to the north and south of the roads) have been arguing that the A344 should be closed, the route returned to grass and traffic diverted along the A303 and that the A303 should be hidden in a long tunnel. With these measures the stone circle would be re-united with the other prehistoric features of this part of the World Heritage Site. Both organisations are also agreed that the present visitor facilities at the site should be removed – and new ones built almost certainly at a location on the edge of the World Heritage Site.

The Department of Transport initially ruled out the long tunnel option as being too expensive and put forward a number of proposals for routes to the north and south. All of these met with strong opposition for a variety of reasons. For example some routes would destroy prime farming land while others would pass too close to the military installations to the north of the site. The Department came under enormous pressure to accept the tunnel option and recently agreed that it is the only viable solution. However, as yet no timescale for upgrading the road has been put forward and the Department has indicated that the tunnel option is too expensive for the foreseeable future. Meanwhile English Heritage is spearheading a bid to the Millennium Commission

to move the visitor facilities to a more suitable location just off the World Heritage Site.

DISCUSSION POINTS: VISITOR FACILITIES

Students could look at the effect visitors have on one particular site, which need not be a World Heritage Site if there is not one within easy access. Are the visitor facilities adequate for the number of visitors? Are there long queues? Are there adequate toilet facilities? What refreshment facilities are there? Is there a commercial outlet? Are the goods it sells appropriate to the site or are they the type of tourist memorabilia that can be bought anywhere in the area? If the latter, does this matter? Are the number of visitors causing other problems on site, for example, overcrowding at particular points or actual erosion of the site? Can your students identify any measures that the site managers have taken to alleviate these problems? Does the site have suggested routeways that are intended to avoid erosion and congestion, as at Fountains Abbey? Are these working?

Students could design a complete new visitor centre or simulate an upgrading of existing facilities, for example, by the provision of disabled access and facilities. They could build models and have a competition as to which design should be used. They could judge the designs themselves or invite a

member of the local planning department or site management team to help them discuss the various merits of the designs. How much will their designs cost? Do they blend in with the local building style as attempted at Fountains? What facilities do they include? Is it possible to use them as visitor attractions in their own right?

If the site suffers from visitor congestion or actual erosion, students could suggest alternative routes or strategies that might protect the site for longer, for example by experimenting with different protective surfaces in busy parts of their schools or colleges. They could also look at some of the wider issues affecting the site – for example, traffic congestion, resulting pollution and present solutions and could use the measures described in the case studies above and in the section on the Athenian Acropolis as examples.

Students could also debate the appropriateness, or even ethics, of surrogate attractions. Should site managers encourage visitors to stay within the confines of a visitor centre – or, in the case of Lascaux, a replica of the cave – or should they encourage them to actually experience the real site? What are the benefits to visitors of visiting a real site? What do they gain from this that they do not get from visiting a replica? If visitors are content with visiting a visitors' centre why not just supply them with a Virtual Reality package through which they could visit the site in the comfort of their own home? If tourism continues to grow at present rates such radical solutions to the physical destruction of sites may be the only way forward. Could a VR display ever take the place of a visit to the real site? Should visiting the real site be restricted to academics, as at Lascaux, or do we all have the right to visit any site we wish, thereby potentially destroying it far more quickly than if access were restricted?

THE PROTECTION OF CULTURAL SITES

THREE COMMON THREATS

Tourism

Tourism can be of great benefit to a site and the area in which it is located. It is essential, however, that tourism is carefully managed so that the cultural and natural aspects of the landscape, and the interests of those who live locally, are properly protected in accordance with the ideal of sustainable tourism accepted by government and by the English Tourist Board. Over-visiting can cause damage both to the landscape (including its wildlife interest) and to individual cultural sites either from erosion or from insensitive development of facilities for visitors. There can also be an adverse effect on farming activities.

Farming

Since the last war, agriculture has gone through enormous and necessary changes. Pressure to intensify land use and to seek greater efficiency has led to the use of new and larger buildings for stock and for storage, and to the amalgamation of farms. There has been a tendency in some areas towards the removal of field boundaries to facilitate the operation of much larger farm machinery and the replacement of old, established walls and ancient hedges by more utilitarian fencing. More immediately, many scheduled archaeological sites are still under the plough and suffering, in some cases significant, damage. There are also places where grazing patterns are causing erosion. All of these aspects of modern farming can affect the setting of cultural sites and many actually affect the conservation of the sites themselves. The way land is used and farmed near to any cultural site needs to be carefully monitored and should become part of any management

The symbol of the World Heritage Convention. The circle stands for nature and the square represents structures built by people. The circle also symbolises the world, with the cupped hands of humankind protecting its cultural and natural heritage. The symbol therefore links the natural and cultural heritage that the Convention protects.

plans developed specifically for World Heritage Sites.

Development

All other types of development near to sites also need careful monitoring. UNESCO now requires each new site to have a *Buffer Zone* which is described as 'an area surrounding the property which has restrictions placed on its use to give an added layer of protection'. The identification of such a zone should help to preserve the setting of any site in a landscape free (as far as possible) from any unnecessary modern intrusions. Two English sites have been threatened recently by inappropriate development.

CASE STUDY: DEVELOPMENT THREATS TO HADRIAN'S WALL

Open-cast mining

A planning application to permit short-term open-cast mining for coal, the restoration of land to agriculture and the provision of a small road materials storage depot within sight of Hadrian's Wall was made to the local authority in 1990. The Authority refused permission on the grounds that:

■ the proposed site was within a County designated Area of Great Landscape Value (AGLV) that

formed part of the setting for Hadrian's Wall and that development would 'create a serious visual intrusion which would be detrimental and contrary to the policies of the County Council to encourage the development of tourism and outdoor recreation'

■ there were 'adequate alternative sources of supply [of coal] available elsewherein the County'.

The Company appealed against this decision and a Public Inquiry was held. In an Inquiry an independent inspector hears evidence from all interested parties and then recommends a course of action to the Secretary of State for the Environment. The Inspector recommended reversing the decision and allowing the development to take place arguing that the short-term nature of the proposed mining would not have a major affect on the AGLV or on the setting of the Wall or on the development of Tourism. However the Secretary of State rejected this advice and refused permission for the mining and other development. He accepted that the designation of Hadrian's Wall as a World Heritage Site did not provide the site with any extra formal legal protection but noted that such designation 'signals the particular importance of that site as a material factor to be taken into account in a planning application'. He therefore considered that *'the Inspector has given insufficient weight to the impact of the proposals on the setting of Hadrian's Wall and the World Heritage Site...the proposals would...be an alien and visually intrusive feature damaging to the setting of Hadrian's Wall and the World Heritage Site'.*

Drilling for gas

A planning application for permission to drill an exploratory bore hole for gas about 400m south of Hadrian's Wall was taken to Public Inquiry in 1991. Despite the short-term nature of the proposal (drilling was only to go on for six weeks) the Inspector recommended the rejection of the application, and in this instance was supported by the Secretary of State, on the grounds that the development would have *'a considerable discordant visual effect when seen from a distance, and dominate the wider archaeological landscape'.*

CASE STUDY: DEVELOPMENT THREATS TO AVEBURY

The part of the World Heritage Site of Stonehenge, Avebury and Associated Megalithic Monuments that clusters around the village of Avebury has been the focus of three recent Public Inquiries. Unlike the above examples from Hadrian's Wall all have been concerned with proposed tourism facilities actually within the area designated as the World Heritage Site.

The first Inquiry decided upon the proposed modified use of an old transport cafe, used mainly by lorry drivers, into a hotel and hostel for visitors to the area. The Ridgeway cafe was on the brow of a hill overlooking a large area of the World Heritage Site and the proposed hotel/hostel would have been visible from the same area. It was also, as its name suggested, immediately adjoining the Ridgeway, an historic routeway and modern public right of way. The proposed hotel/hostel would also have overlooked the Sanctuary, one of the major

archaeological sites that make up the World Heritage Site.

The second Inquiry decided upon a proposed multi-purpose tourism

The entrance to Avebury Manor where visitors were invited to visit a medieval theme park sited somewhat incongruously on the edge of the prehistoric site.

development that was to include a hotel, conference centre, tourist information centre, exhibition facility and separate staff and holiday cottage accommodation. This development was proposed to take place in redundant farm buildings, many of which were listed, at the bottom of the valley partially overlooked by the site of the Ridgeway cafe but essentially hidden from most views.

The third Inquiry decided upon appeals by the owner of Avebury Manor against a number of notices to stop work served by the local authority. The owner of the Manor intended to create a medieval theme park but had started work without receiving planning permission. The Manor, itself an important Listed Building, is sited on the edge of Avebury village within a few hundred metres of the main prehistoric monument.

All three Inquiries refused permission for the proposed developments. In their conclusions all inspectors referred to the designation of Avebury as part of a World Heritage Site and questioned the appropriateness of such developments within the area designated by UNESCO. The debate surrounding the creation of a medieval theme park at Avebury Manor was particularly intense and provoked very high media interest.

The proposal was argued to contravene all of the medium and long term local, regional and national planning and tourism policies covering the area as developed by all of the organisations with such responsibilities, and there was a very vocal opposition group of local residents arguing against the development on the grounds that it would attract thousands of extra tourists who would not only further spoil the peace of the village but who would also contribute to the erosion of the World Heritage Site. However, the local community was actually split over the issue. There was a significant amount of local support from those residents born and bred in the area – as opposed to those who had moved into it – for the scheme as they saw it as stimulating the local economy and providing a much needed source of employment.

The first two Avebury inquiries highlighted the seemingly conflicting requirements of protection of sites and the provision of facilities for tourists drawn to them. In both instances the protectionist arguments were successful. The Avebury Manor Inquiry raised the issue of 'ownership', with a considerable number of local residents supporting a development that sought to take advantage of an existing tourist destination, by chance a World Heritage Site, that would provide a much needed boost to the local economy. Rightly or wrongly, the views of these people were overridden by national and international arguments.

DISCUSSION POINTS: PROTECTION OF SITES

Development threats

Students could take part in a role play exercise simulating a public inquiry called to decide on a proposed development close to a World Heritage Site. They could

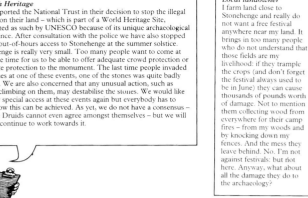

English Heritage
We supported the National Trust in their decision to stop the illegal festival on their land – which is part of a World Heritage Site, designated as such by UNESCO because of its unique archaeological importance. After consultation with the police we have also stopped special out-of-hours access to Stonehenge at the summer solstice. Stonehenge is really very small. Too many people want to come at the same time for us to be able to offer adequate crowd protection or adequate protection to the monument. The last time people invaded the stones at one of these events, one of the stones was quite badly gouged. We are also concerned that any unusual action, such as people climbing on them, may destabilise the stones. We would like to allow special access at these events again but everybody has to agree how this can be achieved. As yet, we do not have a consensus – the Druids cannot even agree amongst themselves – but we will continue to work towards it.

Local landowner
I farm land close to Stonehenge and really do not want a free festival anywhere near my land. It brings in too many people who do not understand that those fields are my livelihood: if they trample the crops (and don't forget the festival always used to be in June) they can cause thousands of pounds worth of damage. Not to mention them collecting wood from everywhere for their camp fires – from my woods and by knocking down my fences. And the mess they leave behind. No, I'm not against festivals: but not here. Anyway, what about all the damage they do to the archaeology?

Druid
We are the descendants of those people who built Stonehenge and other similar monuments. We still follow the ancient, pagan religion of Druidism and feel aggrieved and wronged that we cannot go into our most important temple at the most important time of the year for us. We believe Stonehenge to be our pagan temple; why should we be locked out of our most important place of worship? It is like Christians being locked out of St Paul's Cathedral at Christmas. We do not necessarily agree with many of those who want to hold the festival, as the problems surrounding it have caused us to be excluded from Stonehenge when we want to be there the most.

either use the information given in the examples in this book to develop characters or make up their own scenario – perhaps an inner ring road in Bath, Durham or Edinburgh, or a proposal to convert Blenheim, Durham castle or one of the Welsh castles into a five star hotel. The simulation should illustrate that very few issues are clear cut: development opposed by conservationists may be supported by a range of local individuals and businesses and even visitors who desire a certain level of comfort. If by opposing a given development conservationists stop it will they also succeed in stopping, or at least reducing, visitor numbers? What affect might this have on income that might be used for the conservation of the site?

Inappropriate use of sites

Some World Heritage Sites, for example, Stonehenge, are so famous that they are constantly used for advertising. Students could discuss why a wide range of companies wish to be associated with World Heritage Sites? Should the managers of the sites allow companies to use the sites to promote their products? Companies will often pay quite significant charges for permission to use the image of a site; money that can

then be used for the preservation and presentation of the site. However, many argue that to use a World Heritage Site for, for example, a car advert somehow demeans it. In this case, as in many others, protection does not always have to refer to the physical protection of sites. *Filming and Photography: a matter of respect for the Park and it's people*, a leaflet produced by the managers of Uluru-Kata Tjuta National Park, Australia (and see page 19) clearly illustrates this point:

'Some of the commercial filming and photography that is proposed for the Park is for advertising purposes. As a general rule, such filming will only be allowed if the advertising promotes or enhances the values of the Park, whether cultural, environmental, or social. It will not be permitted if it compromises, detracts or trivialises those values. Any filming must take into account cultural and environmental considerations.'

This stance raises the cultural significance of the site above its possible commercial value. As an extension of this issue students could research the historic and/or

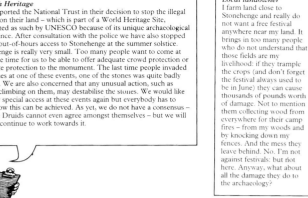

Cardboard huts erected at Great Zimbabwe for a TV documentary about the history of Africa. Site managers are increasingly asked for permission to allow such use of their sites.

A simulation exercise based on the recent troubles at Stonehenge regarding site use and access. (See *A Teacher's Handbook to Stonehenge* for full details).

contemporary religious significance of sites and the effect, if any, that such use has on the management of any particular site. For example, Canterbury Cathedral has an unbroken tradition of Christian worship stretching for over 800 years, a tradition that has a direct affect on the management of modern visitors to the Cathedral (see page 22). The prehistoric sites of Avebury and Stonehenge both seem to have been used for religious purposes for about 1500 years although it is impossible to know whether the beliefs of those who looked after the sites remained constant over all of this time. Since the beginning of this century self-styled so-called Druids have been holding ceremonies at Stonehenge to coincide with the summer solstice. Some groups of these modern Druids claim a religious link to the builders of Stonehenge while other modern Druids protest that Druidism is not a religion at all. The Druid ceremonies (whether religious or not) have become one of the focal points in the debate concerning 'ownership' of the site and who has the right to control access at any given time (see Bibliography and resources: *A Teacher's Handbook to Stonehenge*). Sites could also be used to introduce the idea of respect for the beliefs of others, from Uluru to Canterbury.

Peter Stone

THE NEED FOR LONG-TERM MANAGEMENT

THE NEED FOR MANAGEMENT PLANS

UNESCO's Operational Guidelines require that all World Heritage Sites have management plans. The need for sites to have such plans has also been stressed by the UK government and English Heritage as a means not only of ensuring the preservation and conservation of the sites but also of contributing to the enjoyment and education of visitors and to the development of the idea of sustainable tourism. It is only when site preservation, conservation and presentation strategies are fully integrated with each other within local, regional and national tourism and other development plans that managers can claim to be managing sites properly.

CASE STUDY: HADRIAN'S WALL

There is a particular need to develop a management plan for Hadrian's Wall because of its size and the variety of different land uses to which it is subject. Pressures on the site include the threat of inappropriate development (see pages 29 and 30), poorly managed tourism and the intensification of farming.

Unlike many other World Heritage Sites, the area covered by Hadrian's Wall and its associated features means that it is not managed by one, or even a few managers for conservation purposes. Less than 10% of it is in fact owned in this way. The vast bulk of it is owned and occupied by private individuals or other bodies who, while conscious of and responsive to the needs of conservation, do not have these as their primary objective in the manage-

The Roman fort at Housesteads on Hadrian's Wall is a major tourist attraction.

English Heritage Photo Library

ment of their resources. The World Heritage Site is part of a living and worked-in landscape and has to remain so. In addition to a very large number of owners, the size of the World Heritage Site means that there are also involved over a dozen local authorities with planning, tourism and economic development responsibilities, together with a large number of central government agencies and departments with varying responsibilities for planning, conservation of the natural and cultural environment, access, agriculture and forestry, and for economic development.

The UK Government has decided that World Heritage status does not justify any additional legal controls since there is already an extensive range of protective legislation available for conservation purposes. To be effective in these circumstances, any management plan has to have the tacit assent, at least, of a very large number of individuals and organisations to its objectives and some willingness on their part to use their existing powers and resources to achieve those objectives. Given these

circumstances and the need to conserve the World Heritage Site within a living and worked-in landscape, the Management Plan has to achieve a balance between four major needs.

■ The need to conserve the archaeological sites and their characteristic landscape. The site still has considerable potential to provide further understanding of our past and of the Roman Empire. It is vital, therefore, that the area is managed in such a way as to preserve this finite archaeological evidence.

■ The site lies within a living and working landscape dominated by agricultural activity. An agricultural regime sympathetic to the site and its setting is essential. Their present aspect and the way in which they have evolved over past centuries is largely the result of agricultural activity. If farming did not continue, the changes to the landscape and to the setting of the archaeological remains, as well as to its nature conservation interest, would be drastic and unwelcome. It is important though that any changes in farming are carried out in ways which respect the essential character of the landscape.

■ The need to preserve access to Hadrian's Wall is crucial. The Wall has attracted visitors since at least the sixteenth century and numbers have risen steadily over the last fifty years, although visitor numbers at some major sites seem to have peaked as long ago as 1973. A number of sites are managed by a variety of bodies to provide for public access and there is further access by means of public rights of way, some of which are heavily used. The potential for access will be further increased by the creation of the Hadrian's Wall

National Trail. Public access to the World Heritage Site leading to increased understanding and enjoyment of it is clearly desirable, but must be managed in such a way as to avoid damage to the archaeological sites or to the landscape, and to minimise conflict with other land uses in the World Heritage Site and its setting.

■ The need to consider the contribution made by the World Heritage Site to the regional and national economy. While considerable benefit is derived from farming activity along the length of the Wall, the site can also contribute to the economy through the development of tourism and related services. This contribution has become increasingly important as other industries have declined, and a large number of organisations are looking to tourism to provide an increasing part of the local economy in years to come.

The Preparation of the Management Plan

As the Government's principal advisor on the heritage, English Heritage has taken the lead in the preparation of the Management Plan. However, given the multiple-ownership of the site, it was clear from the outset that obtaining consensus on the Plan's objectives was essential. Thus, from the start a wide range of bodies and individuals, including representatives of farmers and landowners, were involved in the preparation of the Plan. A first consultation draft was issued in July 1995 and over 800 copies were circulated together with 30,000 summary leaflets. A second draft, revised in the light of comments on the first, was published in February 1996 and circulated for comment. This resulted in further amendments of the Plan. A wide-ranging series of consultation meetings with bodies and individuals went on in parallel.

This lengthy consultation process has served two main purposes. First, the eventual document has benefitted from much consideration and is more likely to achieve acceptance. Second, the process of discussion has exposed the issues

---

Guiding principles for management of the Hadrian's Wall World Heritage Site 1996–2026

1.   Provide the opportunity to identify and promote change beneficial to the World Heritage Site and its Setting, and to protect and safeguard their future for coming generations.

2.   Maintain and reinforce the special character of the area.

3.   Retain the vitality of the Wall's landscape.

4.   Maximise public and private resources for the enhancement and management of the landscape.

5.   Use available opportunities to maximise the benefits of sustained long-term management plans of the Wall and its area.

6.   Seize available opportunities for freeing the most sensitive sites from modern development or planting.

7.   Develop understanding of the archaeological or historic value of individual sites and of the World Heritage Site as a whole.

8.   Improve public understanding about the value and importance of the World Heritage Site.

9.   Continue to improve the visitor's visual, cultural, and educational experience of the World Heritage Site.

10. Improve access to and within the Hadrian's Wall World Heritage Site.

11. Ensure that the economic benefits of tourism within the World Heritage Site and its Setting are maximised for the benefit of local communities.

12. Seek to develop partnership and consensus among all those, public or private, involved within the World Heritage Site and its Setting.

---

involved, and the differing viewpoints held, by many of those involved, in a way that had not happened previously. This in itself has helped to develop more receptive attitudes to the need for a Plan and to the problems facing a wide variety of bodies and individuals involved with the site.

The Management Plan

The Plan as finalised proposes a tightly mapped definition for the site. Around this is proposed a *Setting* (or buffer zone), as required by UNESCO, to be agreed with each local authority. The Setting will serve as the basis for planning policies to protect the site in its landscape and also as the area for pro-active support for landscape management schemes which will need to be agreed with landowners and farmers.

The Hadrian's Wall Management Plan runs to 69 pages. Over 800 copies of the first draft of this plan were circulated together with 30,000 summary leaflets in order that everyone who had an interest in the site had an opportunity to comment and influence the final Plan.

The Plan sets out guiding principles for the next thirty years and more specific objectives for the next five years. It also proposes the establishment of a small co-ordination unit for the site to continue to build the consensus and partnerships necessary to make the Plan effective. The unit will be part of English Heritage for at least two years, but will work to a Management Plan Committee which will be made up of all those bodies involved in the area. There will also be a programme of wider communication.

DISCUSSION POINTS: MANAGEMENT AND INTERPRETATION

A wide range of management issues have already been mentioned in the discussion points relating to tourism, visitor facilities and protection of sites. If you look at the Guiding principles for managing Hadrian's Wall (see page 33) you will see that points 8 and 9 refer to visitors' understanding and experience. Much of this will be influenced by the type and amount of interpretation and other information presented to visitors. What kind of information and interpretation should be provided for visitors to World Heritage Sites?

If possible students should visit a World Heritage Site and study both the general information provided to visitors and the site interpretation. Is it immediately clear to a visitor that they are visiting a World Heritage site, and why the site has been so designated?

During a visit students could be given a specified number of photographs (perhaps five) to take to capture essence of the site as it appeared to them. Will they concentrate on the beauty of the overall architecture, on a number of small, particularly impressive or interesting features, or perhaps on the number and type of tourists visiting the site? After the visit the photographs could be mounted in an exhibition with captions explaining why a particular scene has been chosen. Photographs taken or sketches made on site could be developed into abstract art, or as designs for clothing or as a logo for the site or an historic preservation company.

If it is not possible for students to visit a World Heritage Site they could study existing promotional literature for the UK World Heritage Sites or literature produced by UNESCO (see Bibliography and resources). What images are produced for the sites? What aspects of the sites are the leaflets trying promote? Are there regional, national or world messages? What are they? After studying the existing material students could develop their own advertising campaign for a particular site,

writing slogans and other text for the campaign. They could actually design and even produce posters for a campaign to attract visitors to the UK sites or one specific site. Other poster designs could promote the need to conserve

Visitors at Stonehenge use interpretation wands to listen to information about the site thus overcoming the need for intrusive interpretation panels on site.

local/regional/national/world heritage. Students could also design, and possibly produce, site information leaflets or develop tape tour guides, for tourists for a World Heritage Site, perhaps focusing particularly on the needs of disabled or foreign visitors. They could develop this work by producing a storyboard for a video about the site and even produce a real video. After a visit to a World Heritage Site students could draw, paint, or model their reaction to the site.

Some sites could be used as part of a study into architectural styles or garden designs and development. Finally, students could also research past images of the sites: why were they produced? If for 'art' how have styles changed over the years? If for tourism have promotional messages changed?

Given the British Tourism Authority Guidelines for 1993/1997 (see page 24) students could translate existing real material for sites or their own draft documents into foreign languages. They could also prepare a course for custodians at sites that can expect to have large numbers of foreign tourists. What foreign language training would they give staff on a one day course?

An artist's illustration of what Hadrian's Wall might have looked like. Despite the fact that this is only one possible interpretation it is the image that visitors will take away with them.

BIBLIOGRAPHY AND RESOURCES

GENERAL BACKGROUND

Corbishley, M, **Superstructures building the World's great Monuments**, Macdonald Young Books, 1996. ISBN 0-7500-1735-X.

Henson, D, **Teaching Archaeology: a United Kingdom Directory of Resources**, Council for British Archaeology/English Heritage, 1996. ISBN 1-872414-66-4. A comprehensive source book with details of books, audio visual resources, sites, museums and all the relevant addresses.

Swadling, M, (ed), **Masterpieces of Man and Nature: Preserving our World Heritage**, Harper-MacRae, 1992. ISBN 0-646-5376-0.

*von Droste, B, Plachter, H, Rossler, M, **Cultural Landscapes of Universal Value**, Fischer Verlag, 1995.

EDUCATIONAL APPROACHES

While this handbook concentrates on issues of particular relevance to World Heritage Sites, English Heritage has already produced a wide range of handbooks for teachers, tutors and students that deal with site-based work. For a full list of English Heritage educational publications please contact the Education Service (address on page 36).

Alderton, D, **A Teacher's Guide to Using Industrial Sites**, English Heritage, 1995. ISBN 1-85074-445-9.

Anderson, C, Planel, P, and Stone, **A Teacher's Handbook to Stonehenge**, English Heritage, 1996. ISBN 1-85074-312-6.

Cooksey, C, **A Teacher's Guide to Using Abbeys**, English Heritage, 1992. ISBN 1-85074-328-2.

Copeland, T, **A Teacher's Guide to Geography and the Historic Environment**, English Heritage, 1993. ISBN 1-85074-332-0.

Copeland, T, **A Teacher's Guide to Maths and the Historic Environment**, English Heritage, 1992. ISBN 1-85074-329-0.

Copeland, T, **A Teacher's Guide to Using Castles**, English Heritage, 1993. ISBN 1-85074-327-4.

Coupland, L, **A Teacher's Handbook to the Avebury Monuments**, English Heritage, 1988. ISBN 1-85074-173-5.

Durbin, G, **A Teacher's Guide to Using Historic Houses**, English Heritage, 1993. ISBN 1-85074-390-8.

Durbin, G, Morris, M, and Wilkinson, S, **A Teacher's Guide to Learning from Objects**, English Heritage, 1990. ISBN 1-85074-259-6.

Fairclough, J, **A Teacher's Guide to History Through Role Play**, English Heritage, 1994. ISBN 1-85074-333-9.

Keen, J, **A Teacher's Guide to Ancient Technology**, English Heritage, 1996. ISBN 1-85074-448-3.

Keith, C, **A Teacher's Guide to Using Listed Buildings**, English Heritage, 1991. ISBN 1-85074-297-9.

Maddern, E, **A Teacher's Guide to Storytelling at Historic Sites**, English Heritage, 1992. 1-85074-378-9.

Morris, R, and Corbishley, M, **A Teacher's Guide to Churches, Cathedrals, and Chapels**, English Heritage, 1996. 1-85074-447-5.

Pownell, J, & Hutson, N, **A Teacher's Guide to Science and the Historic Environment**, English Heritage, 1992. ISBN 1-85074-331-2.

Scoffam, S, **St Augustine's Abbey: information for teachers**, English Heritage, 1996. free 8 page booklet.

Watson, I, **A Teacher's Handbook to Hadrian's Wall**, English Heritage, 1997. ISBN 1-85074-375-4.

For information about educational resources and visits and general publications regarding other World Heritage Sites please contact the Site direct.

UNESCO PUBLICATIONS

*The World Heritage Map A wallchart including a world map indicating the position of all World Heritage Sites and brief information on various aspects of the Convention.

*The World Heritage List The complete List of World Heritage Sites including the criteria under which the sites were inscribed on the List.

*Brief descriptions of World Heritage Sites Short descriptions of all sites on the World Heritage List.

*The World Heritage (leaflet) Brief description of the Convention and its workings.

*Convention concerning the Protection of the World Cultural and Natural Heritage The full text of the Convention as adopted by UNESCO in 1972.

*Operational Guidelines for the Implementation of the World Heritage Convention The full Operational Guidelines to which all site managers must comply.

**The World Heritage Desk Diary Annual diary with illustrations of World Heritage Sites and information about the Convention etc.

Below: Silbury Hill, the largest artificial mound in Europe, and part of the Stonehenge/Avebury World Heritage Site. Despite three excavations its original function remains unclear.

Right: The facade of West Kennet Long Barrow, also one of the monuments of the Stonehenge/Avebury World Heritage Site. The remains of over 47 people were found during excavations in the 1950s. The problem of visitor erosion can be clearly seen at the entrance to the barrow.

Opposite page: The first glimpse of the remains of El-Khazneh or 'Pharaoh's treasury' at Petra, Jordan from the siq. The building was in fact a tomb built for a Nabataean king, probably in the first century BC. (Peter Stone)

**The World Heritage A series of publications for students aged 8–15.

**The World Heritage Review A quarterly magazine with in-depth articles on World Heritage Sites and issues.

* available free of charge from: The UNESCO World Heritage Centre
7 Place de Fontenoy
75352 Paris 07
France

** available from:
The UNESCO Publishing Office
1 rue Miollis
75732 Paris Cedex 15
France
Information concerning the World Heritage is also available from UNESCO through the INTER-NET:
http://www.unesco.org/whc/ or gopher://gopher.unesco.org/11/Heritage

ICOMOS UK PUBLICATIONS

A range of publications suitable for background informationfor teachers and older students:

Heritage and Tourism, Conference papers, ICOMOS, 1990, ISBN 0-9517677-1-2.

Management of World Heritage Sites, Seminar papers, ICOMOS,1991, ISBN 0-9517677-0-4.

Cultural Landscapes, Seminar papers, ICOMOS, 1994, ISBN 0-9517677-6-3.

English World Heritage Sites Monitoring Reports 1995, ICOMOS, 1995, ISBN 0-9517677-7-1.

Historic Cities and Sustainable Tourism, Conference papers, ICOMOS, 1995, ISBN 0-9517677-08-X.

All available for purchase from ICOMOS UK, 10 Barley Mow Passage, London, W4 4PH.

Acknowledgements

Henry Cleere, Sarah Craighead, David Earlam, Terry Frazier, Cornelia Hadziaslani, Gwilym Hughes, John Jameson, Linda Martin, Dino Milinović, Steve More, Stephanie Moser, Ivan Murambiwa, Edward Nutanga, Breda Pavlic, Dino Politis, Philip Whitbourn.

Our Education Service aims to help teachers make better use of the historic environment. We welcome educational parties free of charge to over 400 historic sites cared for by English Heritage. A free introductory booklet, **Visiting Historic Sites and Buildings** and a **Resources** catalogue are available on request. We also run **Windows on the Past**, a special membership scheme for teachers. For further details contact:

**English Heritage
Education Service
429 Oxford Street
London
W1R 2HD**

**Tel: 0171-973 3442
Fax: 0171 973 3443**